MODELLING
European Railways

MODELLING
European Railways

Peter Marriott

THE CROWOOD PRESS

First published in 2016 by
The Crowood Press Ltd
Ramsbury, Marlborough
Wiltshire SN8 2HR

www.crowood.com

British Library Cataloguing-in-Publication Data
A catalogue record for this book is available from the British Library.

ISBN 978 1 78500 126 0

Disclaimer
The author and the publisher do not accept any responsibility in any manner whatsoever for any
error or omission, or any loss, damage, injury, adverse outcome, or liability of any kind incurred
as a result of the use of any of the information contained in this book, or reliance upon it. If in
doubt about any aspect of railway modelling readers are advised to seek professional advice.

Typeset and designed by D & N Publishing, Baydon, Wiltshire.

Printed and bound in Malaysia by Times Offset (M) Sdn Bhd.

CONTENTS

ACKNOWLEDGEMENTS

Thanks go to numerous folk who have made modelling European railways a lot of fun for me, including David Aldis, Hansueli Kunz, Ian Futers, Stewart Gorman and Pelle Søeborg.

For those who have contributed to this book I must add my profuse gratitude, because their contributions have added to the scope of the book. These include John Atkinson, who knows so much more about operating railways to a timetable than I had imagined was possible. Paul Smith, who shares with us in these pages his excellent N-, HO- and O-scale layouts and expertise. Peter Brett of Winco kindly read the chapters on models and high-speed trains so that I could ensure that I was as up to date as possible regarding availability of models. Stephan Kraus allowed me to take pictures of his various layouts, which has enhanced the narrow-gauge aspects of this book. Chris Nevard positioned some of my rolling stock on his superb layouts and then ably took marvellous pictures of them. Norman Lamb and other members of the Austrian Railway Group gave very helpful comments on the Case Study chapter.

Thanks also to Stewart Gorman for lending me his SNCF rolling stock on occasions and to David Aldis for letting me work on his N-scale Swiss-based layout.

For those who have accompanied me on various European railway jaunts I thank John Atkinson, Geoff Crossland, David Brown and Les Heath. All those trips were a lot of fun!

Thanks go to my wife Mary who has to put up with living with little bits of Europe dotted around our house. I really do appreciate her patience and long suffering!

As soon as this book is published, I am sure I will immediately recall the names of many others who have helped me and I say thank you to those too.

ILLUSTRATION CREDITS

My thanks go to the photographers and model-makers who agreed that I could use some of their pictures and layouts in this book:

- Stephan Kraus, who is a professional layout builder in Germany offering diorama and layout-building services plus modelling seminars at www.modellbau-smk.de
- Chris Nevard, *Model Rail*'s ace photographer, who always brings the best out in my layouts through his photographic expertise
- Busch and its agents in the UK, Golden Valley Hobbies, for the pictures of its products
- Noch and its agents in the UK, Gaugemaster, for the pictures of its scenery products.

In addition, I say thank you to model railway editors who have published words and pictures about my layouts over the past decades and who have agreed that snippets of some of those layouts can be portrayed within this book:

- Andrew Burnham of *Continental Modeller*
- Stephen Ford of *Austrian Railway Group Journal*
- Malcolm Bulpitt of *Swiss Express*
- Bruno Kalbrerer and Martin Meyenburg of the Swiss *LOKI* magazine.
- Dennis Lovett of *Bachmann Times*
- David Brown, late of *International Railway Modelling*, for his support in my early years of model railway journalism
- Ben Jones, now of *British Railway Modelling*, who has published numerous articles of my European layouts during his spell at *Model Rail International* magazine
- Richard Foster, as editor of *Model Rail* magazine, who continues to pore over my words and pictures each month and turns them into something that looks better in the magazine than in reality.

CHAPTER ONE

WHY MODEL EUROPEAN RAILWAYS?

What attracts modellers to build a European-inspired layout?

For many people, European railways have an attraction that the railways of the United Kingdom cannot match – they prefer to model the railways of countries that they visit on holiday, or that they want to visit, or they may be looking for a new challenge after years of modelling UK layouts. In this first chapter, we will identify some of the features of European railways that modellers find appealing.

ABOVE: **Shunting wagons in timber loading yard in HO scale using SNCF Fret motive power.**

RIGHT: **The Gotthard route is very popular with modellers and railway enthusiasts, though from the end of 2016 most of the traffic on the Gotthard line will use the base AlpTransit Tunnel. Here is a model of part of the line using scenery products by Heki displayed at the Nuremberg Toy Fair.**

WHAT MAKES EUROPEAN RAILWAYS ATTRACTIVE FOR MODELLERS?

The European railway network includes standard, narrow and broad gauges operated by private and nationally owned railway companies. Its railway routes range from recently built high-speed corridors to rural single-track branches climbing mountain slopes with the assistance of rack systems. It is true that the UK has a similar variety of railway systems (apart from broad gauge), but it cannot arguably compete with the sheer volume of different European railway systems.

Standard- and narrow-gauge railway networks frequently operate side by side and for example at Jenbach in Austria standard-gauge OBB (Austrian State Railways) and two different narrow-gauge railways operate from the same station. Another example from Switzerland is Interlaken Ost, where standard-gauge SBB locomotives share platforms with the privately owned BLS. Cross-platform connections take passengers to the metre-gauge Zentralbahn line over the Brünig Pass to Lucerne and the Bernese Oberland Bahn (BOB) network of lines, culminating in the highest railway station in Europe

at Jungfraujoch. In addition, within half a kilometre of Interlaken Ost station there is a funicular railway to Harder Kulm.

Border stations have a special excitement of their own, with motive power and rolling stock of more than one country arriving and departing. Prestige EuroCity passenger services thread across the rail networks of Europe and cross national borders frequently, with trains often composed of carriages from several countries and sometimes involving changes of locomotives at border stations.

The departure boards at major European stations list domestic and cross-European destinations that conjure appealing ideas of rail travel. The names Orient Express and Glacier Express carry with them images of luxury carriages, superb food and wine, glamorous passengers and legendary destinations. Train names such as the EuroCity Transalpin, City Night Line Andromeda, Thalys Soleil and Trenhotel Sud Expresso maybe have more appeal than the 17.27 from London Waterloo to Alton.

European locomotive liveries are certainly more varied than the familiar English, Welsh & Scottish (EWS) red and gold livery that is seen in the UK, because as open-access private companies continue

Busch offers great potential for narrow-gauge modelling with its mining railway system and Feldbahn (Field Railway). The HOf scale system uses a track system of 6.5mm rail gauge with a central magnetic strip that runs centrally between the rails and can be disguised by ballast. There are starter sets, plus a number of different wagons. BUSCH

RIGHT: *HOm-gauge layouts are very popular for those who like the Swiss metre-gauge lines. Bemo caters well for this market sector along with Peco, which manufactures HOm track. Here, a Bemo RhB Ge 4/4 I number 601 clings to the side of a narrow ledge.*

BELOW LEFT: *A French country station modelled in HO scale, with an X73500 'Whale' diesel single-car unit by Jouef offering the local passenger service.*

ABOVE RIGHT: *The romance of Europe's classic long-distance expresses is captured in this detail on an HO-scale Orient Express carriage by Rivarossi. Maybe Hercule Poirot is on board?*

LEFT: *A DB V160 Bo-Bo locomotive on the Brawa demonstration layout at the 2009 Nuremberg Toy Fair.*

Carriage destination notices such as this convey the excitement of a European railway journey.

Class 460 main-line locos feature a wide variety of colour schemes from Kambly biscuits to Western Union, while in Austria Taurus locos carry numerous colours. Often Diesel Multiple Units (DMUs) and Electric Multiple Units (EMUs) such as the French X72500 units and Austrian Talent units carry regional colours.

Various European rail companies still use mixed trains and some narrow-gauge networks 'piggy-back' standard-gauge wagons on narrow-gauge wagons. Shunting of rolling stock in the UK is becoming increasingly limited to freight operations, but in mainland Europe motorail trains, sleeper carriages, mixed trains, the adding and subtracting of carriages and the division of trains en route leads to frequent shunting operations. Sadly, the sleeper train network in Europe seems to be reducing year on year, although there are still some notable exceptions, including the Moscow to Nice sleeper and Thello services operating between France and Italy. There are also overnight services from Spain using Talgo rolling stock.

to enter railway operation the range of colourful liveries increases still further. In addition, many national railway companies permit locos to carry full advertising liveries. For example, many Swiss railways (SBB)

Privately operated freight and passenger services are now increasingly seen across Europe. This HO-scale Vossloh G1206 loco by Mehano carries the Veolia livery.

Operating between Hamburg and Copenhagen on a daily basis are various EuroCity trains that use the train ferry from Puttgärden. Diesel DB (Deutsche Bahn – German Railways) Inter-City Express (ICE) and DSB (Danske Statsbaner – Danish Railways) Inter-City (IC) train sets drive on to the ferry for a 45-minute sea crossing between Germany and Denmark.

Multiple-unit trains are becoming the mainstay of Europe's passenger services, but there are still many regular locomotive-hauled passenger services. There are also still plenty of locomotive movements at many of the larger stations in Europe.

Many cities, including Innsbruck in Austria, Bordeaux in France and Amsterdam in the Netherlands, operate extensive tram networks. Trams, the track, road inserts, tram stops and catenary are all available in model form in various scales.

ABOVE: **To the right the conifer tree by Busch has cones added for even more realism. The ferns are plastic leaves also by Busch. The signal is by Schneider, the ÖBB Class 1044 locomotive by Roco, the catenary by Viessmann and the lineside plants by miniNatur.**

RIGHT: **Modern and classic tram networks are dotted across Europe. This one is in the French city of Montpellier.**

AVAILABILITY OF MODELS

There is a huge selection of good quality ready-to-run European railway models to tempt our credit cards. The detail on the models and their running qualities are generally of very high standards and these railway models are supported by an enormous scenic and accessory industry.

European model railway manufacturers are keen to lead the trends within the hobby; for example, laser-cut technology is being expanded by European kit manufacturers. Big brands are encouraging children to take up railway modelling – Faller's Basic and Roco's New Generation are just two of the current initiatives.

*ABOVE: **Nothing attracts attention at a model railway exhibition quite like a large-scale steam locomotive fitted with DCC sound.***

*LEFT: **A seated passenger awaiting the next service to Lyon. He has parked his Jeep in the station car park.***

Roco and other companies are trying to be forward-looking in the hobby to attract new younger members into the hobby. Here, Roco's Z21 digital control system is being promoted along with a New Generation theme of basic train sets.

Some European manufacturers are trying very hard to attract new members into the hobby, including children. Faller has its Basic brand to appeal to younger people.

THE CHANNEL ADDS FURTHER VARIETY

Eurostar has sparked interest in European railways among the general public that is continuing to grow. Europe is now accessible by rail, rather than only by ferry, hovercraft or air. One only has to visit the splendid London St Pancras International station to feel the excitement of trans-European rail travel. From May 2015, Eurostar is running direct trains to destinations in the south of France from London in addition to its regular services to Brussels, Lille and Paris.

The building and operation of the Channel Tunnel brought together the operation of British and European passenger rolling stock. Eurostar trains operate on designated lines in the UK, Belgium and France and in the near future new Eurostar trains are to enter service that are anticipated to work directly between the UK and the Netherlands and Switzerland. DB has future plans to use some of its ICE sets for direct services between the UK and Germany through the Tunnel.

During the Channel Tunnel construction project BR Class 08 and 20 locos worked alongside French and German locos and for the first few months of Tunnel freight operations French Class 222xxx locos worked freight trains into the UK. Since the building of the Channel Tunnel, UK Class 20, 37, 56, 58 and 66 locomotives have worked in Europe on the building of various new high-speed lines, including those in France and Spain.

UK motive power meets French motive power at Annemasse, France, on 11 November 2008. Some of the EWS Class 66 locomotives have seen service in mainland Europe and in addition various UK-based Class 20, 37, 56 and 58 locomotives have seen action on Europe's new high-speed line projects.

After the successful test run through the Channel Tunnel on the previous weekend, DB presented an ICE 406 in London for the first time on 19 October 2010. ICE services are planned between London and Frankfurt via Cologne, Brussels and Lille. This will include connections from London to Amsterdam via Rotterdam. The journey time from London to Cologne should take less than four hours and from London to Frankfurt just over five hours. Journeys from London to Amsterdam should be possible in less than four hours.

CONCLUSIONS

Any who have modelled UK railways for some years may be a looking for a new project and a challenge to rekindle their modelling enthusiasm. For inspiration, there is no need to look further than across the English Channel, because most countries are within reasonable travelling time and the so-called budget airlines make research opportunities fairly cheap. Reproducing part of the railway delights of a rural branch line in Italy or the Alpine lines of Austria or Slovenia may make a refreshing change from modelling a 1980s suburban line or a GWR branch line in the UK.

One problem the modeller might have is that unless he has a favourite country or line, the choice of railways and countries in Europe to model is huge. However, there are a good number of UK-based enthusiast societies covering most European countries and these provide an excellent way to learn more about the railways of the country of your choice. Their magazines, forums, model railway shows and ability to be in touch with like-minded enthusiasts are all fun ways to learn about the prototype railway and what is available for the modeller.

In Europe, many modellers choose to build well-detailed dioramas and modules rather than huge layouts. These modules then form part of an integrated modular layout instead of having a full personal layout. These modellers have concluded that building something is better than dreaming of an extensive layout that will not get built and of course any experience gained while building a diorama will provide sufficient

Roco ÖBB Class 2045 crosses a viaduct built from a Kibri plastic kit.

Leaflets of just four of the UK-based European railway modelling societies.

LEFT: *Cameo scenes can be made, such as this permanent-way team working from a BLS Tm 235 Robel vehicle with a crane. The unmotorized fully assembled vehicle is by Kibri, though motorized versions are available in N and HO scale from Hobbytrade and Viessmann.*

confidence to tackle something more ambitious in the future.

The words and pictures in this book will hopefully encourage modellers to commence work on a European railway modelling project. It may remind you of a past holiday, or maybe it will be a taster of a future holiday to come. Whatever it is, enjoy modelling European railways.

LEFT: *Close-up of the HO-scale permanent-way workers by Preiser. I dribbled a little weathering dye over the figures to create the illusion of dirty work gear.*

BELOW: *A Traxx locomotive in Zebra livery No. 666 by Piko in HO scale. The catenary is by Hornby International and the tunnel mouth and the retaining wall by Noch. There is now a huge range of scenic materials for every season that are available to represent grasses, weeds and vegetation for every European location.*

BOTTOM: *O scale is becoming very popular with modellers across Europe. Here is a scene on the Lenz exhibition layout seen at a recent toy fair in Nuremberg.*

CHAPTER TWO

RESEARCHING EUROPEAN RAILWAYS

How does one start to learn about European railways?

Some delay beginning to model European railways because they think it is essential to know at least one European language, but this is not so. Many who model European railways do not speak European languages and there is an excellent choice of avenues of research that do not require fluent German or French, for example.

Joining the society of your chosen European prototype is a very good way to expand your knowledge. Their annual subscriptions are comparatively low and represent good value for money to find out more about a particular country's railway operations and their magazines often contain information in English about prototype and modelling developments. Some railway societies have lists of railway terms in English of their appropriate language available for members. If the society holds an AGM and exhibition, these are good places to meet with fellow enthusiasts and to learn about the latest developments in the railway activity of the country.

VIDEOS

Video recordings are a very important and valuable source of research. Views from the cab, at the lineside, from helicopters and inside the trains are just some of the vantage points available to the viewer on these productions. There are various specialist video productions available from a number of sources in the UK, including Ticket to Ride and Lineside Video Productions, with MITV producing its own range of Swiss productions and stocking videos from other companies. The Lineside Video Productions series entitled *European Railway* is particularly useful because its quarterly productions feature a selection of the

DVD recordings are a great way to learn more about Europe's railways. There are driver's-eye view videos, scenes from the lineside and helicopter footage. To supplement these, YouTube has a huge selection of video recordings by amateur and professional photographers.

railways of European countries (www.linesidevideos.co.uk).

Some BBC television documentaries feature European lines, including the popular *Great Railway Journeys of the World*, Michael Portillo's railway programmes and Michael Palin's *Around the World in 80 Days*.

USING THE INTERNET

Increasingly, YouTube videos are available on the Internet covering almost anywhere in Europe that you may choose to learn about. One Internet site that contains a huge range of information that is useful to modellers following the European scene is www.railfaneurope.net, with its wealth of links, railway maps, livery information and stock lists.

The Internet has a vast array of information, including national rail information, model manufacturers and enthusiast sites, and some of these are listed in the Appendices. Many more can be accessed via links and search engines and many of the European Internet railway sites have text and information in English.

Fewer and fewer European rail operators produce their own timetables in book form each year and increasingly rail travellers use the Internet to search for train times. One recommended website with a good European-wide timetable search facility is www.bahn.co.uk. The www.seat61.com website is a splendid source of information about rail travel covering most European countries.

VISITING EUROPE

It goes without saying that the best way to undertake research is to visit the area of your choice and travel on the trains that you wish to model. European package tours offer coach, air, fly-drive and specific rail holidays. Camping deals that include the Channel crossing and use of a 'luxury' tent are one of the cheaper options. Many travellers today choose to book their own flights and accommodation on the Internet and European rail tickets can be purchased using a number of websites, including Voyages SNCF (www.uk.voyages-sncf.com/en), which was previously known as Rail Europe. The so-called budget airlines, including Airberlin, easyJet, flybe, Germanwings, Ryanair and Wizz Air offer potentially good value flights to a wide choice of destinations from many local airports provided that you book the flights long enough in advance to take advantage of the best fares.

If you prefer to travel in a group there are several specialist companies offering European rail tours designed for the enthusiast and those who just like travelling by rail including Ffestiniog Travel (www.myrailtrip.co.uk), Rail Europe (www.rail-europe.co.uk), PTG Tours (www.ptg.co.uk) and Stars International Tours (www.stars-tours.org.uk).

Do not limit research simply to the railway operations of European countries, because architecture and building styles need to be observed along with signalling systems, the landscape, types of vegetation, agricultural crops grown, the seasonal changes, breeds of animals, motor transport and so on. The scope for potential research is endless, but it will all contribute to the overall realism of a layout.

Traxx locomotives by Bombardier are seen extensively across Europe. DB Class 189 904 carries the Zebra livery of Rail Traction Company and is standing at Brenner with a northbound freight service on 13 July 2012.

ABOVE: **The distinctive yellow and blue livery of NS (Nederlandse Spoorwegen – Netherlands Railways) on loco 1770 and carriages at Maastricht on 4 April 2007.**

LEFT: **Classic French semaphore signals at Aix en Provence on 12 November 2006. Similar signals are still in use today in some parts of France, though with the passage of time colour light signals are replacing most of them.**

BOOKS AND MAPS

Books about European railways can be obtained from book suppliers, including Amazon, Ian Allan and Platform 5 Publishing. Many of the books contain good pictorial content with (occasionally) some text and/or captions in English. Do not be put off buying books in other languages, because it is surprising how quickly one picks up the meaning of common terms in the picture captions and the text. Motive-power handbooks, with full English text, covering various European countries are retailed by Platform 5

Publishing Ltd (52 Broadfield Road, Sheffield S8 0XJ or telephone 0114 255 8000).

There are numerous European guidebooks, but some are better than others for rail-oriented travellers. The Bradt rail guides that cover Greece, Russia, the Eurostar cities (Paris, Brussels and Lille) and Switzerland are useful for those countries (for more information about Bradt books go to www.bradtguides.com). In my experience, Lonely Planet and Rough Guide books also offer good historical, geographical, accommodation and travel information for the rail-based traveller.

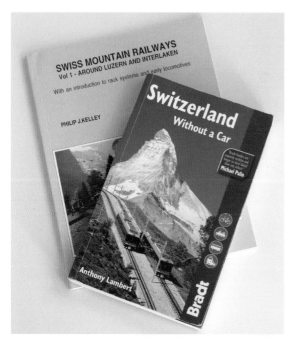

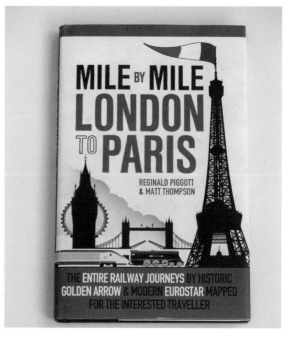

ABOVE LEFT: **The most popular countries among modellers in the UK following the European scene appear to be Austria, Germany and Switzerland. These countries are very well catered for with books, magazines, enthusiast societies and lots of models of everything needed to make a superb and accurate model railway.**

ABOVE RIGHT: **Eurostar journeys that are now routine can be made more interesting by line guides such as this one.**

The monthly paper *European Rail Timetable* contains details of the main current passenger rail services. Branch lines and feeder stopping routes are also mentioned briefly, together with special features in alternate issues, including sample fares, cruise trains and rail holidays, rail passes, tourist railways, high-speed trains and night trains. In addition, there are summer and winter timetables that include additional useful travel information. These timetables are no longer produced by Thomas Cook, but are now independently produced by the team who used to produce the Thomas Cook publication. For more information go to: www.europeanrailtimetable.eu.

The *Thomas Cook* European Rail Timetable (ERT) ceased production in summer 2014, but fortunately its production staff have now reintroduced the timetable on a monthly basis. Both the Austrian and Swiss railway groups produce superb area guides in the English language as an introduction for visitors and enthusiasts.

The monthly paper **European Rail Timetable** *contains details of the main current passenger rail services.*

There are several European rail atlases available. This selection by Schweers and Wall is pictorially very clear and detailed and has an EU atlas, plus others that just cover one country. These are available on Amazon and at book retailers in the UK.

It will be worth obtaining at least one railway map of Europe. The Thomas Cook European Rail Map is a good overview map of the main lines and it usefully identifies some of the scenic journeys. There are a few maps produced by the Quail Map Company that include a Greece Railway Map containing some historical information. Stanfords often stocks rail maps of various countries at its London bookshop. The German company, Schweers and Wall, produces some very clear European Rail Atlases, with one covering the EU and others covering Austria, Germany and Switzerland. One website that contains a large number of atlases for purchase is www.europeanrailwayatlas.com.

News-stand magazines with English text about European railways include *Continental Railway Journal, Today's Railways Europe, Continental Modeller, Modern Railways, Railway Magazine* and others. Personally, I find that *Today's Railways Europe* is a good all-round source of current information Europe-wide. These can be

Another selection of rail atlases and maps that is quite easy to obtain from the main stations in Europe and from Stanfords bookshops in the UK.

supplemented by the specialist society magazines. In addition, there are numerous European magazines, including *Mondo Ferroviaria, Eisenbahn Journal, LOKI, MIBA, Eisenbahn Amateur, Le Train, Loco Revue, Modelspoormagazine, Rail Miniature Flash* and many others.

ABOVE LEFT: **The amount of information readily available in the UK in printed form about Europe's railways is good, with** Today's Railways Europe **leading the way for prototype information.** Modern Railways **features selected highlights each month and** Continental Modeller **covers the worldwide modelling scene.**

ABOVE RIGHT: **Large newsagents in Germany are awash with good-quality monthly and quarterly publications about European model railways. Here are just three of the most familiar magazines.**

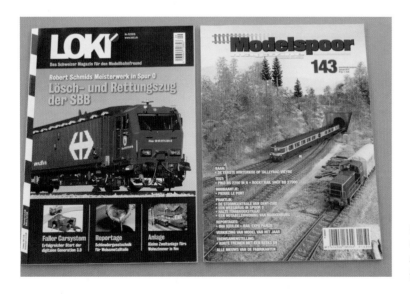

In Switzerland, **LOKI** *magazine covers both prototype and model subjects.* **Modelspoor** *magazine is published in Belgium.*

Most of the model railway shows in the UK now include one or more European layouts and some shows, such as the Warley National Model Railway Exhibition at the NEC in Birmingham, feature an entire section devoted to non-UK layouts. In addition to these general shows, there are some that are made up of only European layouts coupled with a profusion of retailers specializing in European models and society stands. These are the ideal places to gain inspiration and find out what is on offer for the European enthusiast. Visiting one of the main model railway shows in Europe is another good way to learn more. For example, the On traXS show in Utrecht, the Netherlands, is accessible from many UK local airports for the day via Amsterdam Airport Schipol and a train journey from the airport.

Tourist offices of most European countries will be happy to supply maps and colour brochures about the country, its towns and travel facilities. Some may be able to provide route timetables and general rail network information. Increasingly this information is downloadable from their websites.

RAILWAY FOOTPATHS

Some railway companies build footpaths so that families and enthusiasts can watch passing trains at scenic locations. At least two Swiss railway companies have done this – the BLS and the Rhätische Bahn (RhB).

The BLS Kander Valley Eisenbahn Erlebnis-Pfad for railway enthusiasts and walkers was opened in 1993 as a Railway Adventure Trail between Blausee Mitholz and Kandergrund on the Lötschberg line. The walk is signposted throughout, with various information boards along the path giving information about the BLS line, its operations and the area. An English interpretation of the boards is available in (free) leaflet form from the main BLS stations in the area. The path

winds its way alongside and under the main line, providing superb views of both the railway activities and the beautiful Kander Valley. The walk, which is open between the end of April and October, takes about an hour. Some of the metal staircases may be a little daunting to those who fear heights and good walking shoes are recommended. To join the route, alight the train at Frutigen or Kandersteg, then transfer to a local bus to Blausee or Kandergrund. Brown signs mark the route of the railway path, which in 2013 the BLS fully opened between Brig and Frutigen.

RhB Lehrpfad is the Rhätische Bahn Historic Railway Path between Preda and Bergün on the Albula line. The walk is signposted throughout, with various information boards (in German) giving information about the Rhätische Bahn. The path provides superb views of the line, its viaducts and the beautiful Albula Valley. During the first part of the descent from Preda, the railway is more visible than in the second part of the walk. Preda is 1,788m above sea level and Bergün is 1,372m above sea level, so normally walkers use the path for the descent rather than the ascent. The 8km walk, which is open between the end of May and October, takes about two hours. Good walking shoes are recommended, because the path is rocky in places and there are some fairly steep climbs, although these are relatively short.

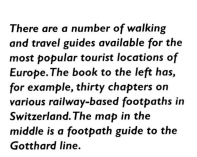

There are a number of walking and travel guides available for the most popular tourist locations of Europe. The book to the left has, for example, thirty chapters on various railway-based footpaths in Switzerland. The map in the middle is a footpath guide to the Gotthard line.

Trees sometimes shade the path and at other times it crosses meadows, with seats being provided at various locations along the route. For a plan of the route pick up a copy of the *RhB Wander-Erlebnis* leaflet.

CATALOGUES

Auhagen, Bemo, Busch, Faller, Fleischmann, Fulgurex, HAG, Kibri, LGB, Liliput, Märklin, Noch, Rivarossi, Roco and other manufacturers produce catalogues that generally contain good colour photographs of both model and occasionally prototype locomotives, rolling stock and buildings. The latest catalogues from these main players are sometimes bulky, but their annual new-release brochures following the January Nuremberg Toy Fair are usually free of charge from retailers.

Bemo's catalogue is a first-class introduction to Swiss European narrow-gauge modelling, picturing its HOm and HOe ranges and including photographs of the prototype. Various layouts are pictorially featured, which is inspirational, and the text is multilingual, including English. Bemo also produces a magazine called *Bemo Post* several times a year that includes details of new and pending product releases and layouts featuring Bemo products.

DAY TRIPS TO EUROPE

Over the past eight years, I have taken around twenty day trips to Europe whenever I wanted to remind myself how the European railway scene looks. Well, the truth is that I just enjoy planning and going on such trips. I am fortunate to live about thirty minutes' drive away from London Luton Airport, which has an enormous number of daily flights to many European countries. For those living near London Heathrow or Gatwick there is an even greater frequency of flights and variety of destinations available. Gone are the days when you could fly to and from Europe for less than £20 – I did that seven times – but it is still possible to obtain return flights to places such as Geneva for £60 if you book up well in advance.

Alternatively, Eurostar offers an easy way to spend a day in Belgium or France for around £70 from London St Pancras International station. If you want to explore the Belgian rail network opt for its add-on Anywhere in Belgium ticket for an extra £10 at the time of booking. The ticket includes onward and in-bound travel on any trains in Belgium on your days of travel apart from ICE or Thalys high-speed trains.

With an early departure and a late return flight it is possible to get up to ten hours to explore rail journeys. A similar time abroad is possible on Eurostar journeys by using the first out and last back trains. The one disadvantage with these day trips is that by 3pm you may be feeling rather tired if you had a very early wake-up call. For this reason, some enthusiasts either choose to stay at a hotel on the airport the evening before, or extend the trips to two days. From personal experience, I find that having a good breakfast at the airport or Eurostar terminal is the best way to keep one's energy levels up during the day. That and some coffee and chocolate during the day!

It is well worth doing some advance research about local transport passes of your chosen destination. One good source of such information is the *Today's Railways Europe* magazine supplement given away with the June issue of the magazine. The www.seat61.com website is another splendid source of information on rail travel covering most European countries and is well worth consulting before you go. The SNCF Voyages website and other websites provide the opportunity to purchase rail tickets before you leave the country.

Use the Internet to download local rail timetables and network maps before you travel and those travelling with smartphones or tablets can upload the documents and apps before departure. Many European rail operators offer a timetable facility for smartphones that have the roaming activated in Europe.

If landing at Geneva Airport, as you leave the arrivals hall look out for the ticket machine that dispenses a ticket for free travel in the Geneva conurbation for an hour. This gives you sufficient time to get to the main station, where a selection of French and Swiss trains will be seen, plus time to travel to one or two of the local suburban stations.

The websites and in-flight magazines of the airline that you fly on will explain how to travel from the airport to the main railway stations. Some have designated shuttle buses and others are served by trams. Some of

the main airports are rail-served, including Amsterdam, Cologne Bonn, Frankfurt, Geneva, Milan Malpensa, Munich, Vienna and Zürich, which means that you will be travelling on trains within a few minutes of your landing if the queue at the passport desk is not too long.

Visiting a European model railway exhibition is a good way of combining seeing local rail services plus a visit to a show. Some shows are held in major exhibition centres that are well served from airports.

TOP: *This on-platform refreshment stall at Geneva main station captures the excitement of European rail travel with its list of famous European cities.*

RIGHT: *Classic German steam loco 58 311 in September 2006 at a special event in the Black Forest.*

Ostend station on 15 July 2009 with SNCB locomotive 1358 awaiting its next duty. There is still plenty of locomotive movement at many of Europe's stations.

Modernized German local terminus station with two Regio Shuttle units (made by Stadler) awaiting to depart. Models of these units are available in HO scale from Bemo and Roco.

Wagonload freight traffic is still witnessed across Europe. Here at Langnau in the Emmental area of Switzerland diesel locomotive SBB Am 843 082 shunts wagons with refuse containers on 26 May 2010.

One of France's most scenic lines is through the Cevennes region. Here, SNCF 567601 stands at the head of a short train of classic carriages on an excursion train on 10 June 2010.

SWISS TRAVEL PASS

Launched twenty-five years ago for visitors to Switzerland, this popular way to explore the country includes unrestricted travel by train, bus and boat on over 27,000km nationwide, 50 per cent off most of the mountain railways and unlimited travel on municipal public transport in seventy-five towns and cities. In addition, it covers admission to 480 museums throughout the country. The Swiss Travel Pass is valid for three, four, eight or fifteen days.

For those wanting flexibility, the Swiss Travel Pass Flex offers travel on public transport on any of three, four, eight or fifteen freely selectable days within a one-month period. A Swiss Half Fare Card Combi gives more opportunities too. Travellers under the age of twenty-six can purchase either the Swiss Travel Pass Youth or Swiss Travel Pass Flex Youth at 15 per cent discount off the regular ticket price.

In addition, the Swiss Transfer Ticket (travel from any Swiss airport or border railway station to any holiday destination in Switzerland and back) and a one-month Swiss Half Fare Card (offering up to 50 per cent reduction off travel on Swiss public transport) are available.

To see more about the Swiss Travel Pass go to: www.swisstravelsystem.com. The website contains details of all the available tickets, suggested routes and offers. The Ticket Finder facility is a useful way to choose the best value for money ticket for you.

For a huge amount of information about Switzerland including its railways go to www.myswitzerland.com.

Day trip to Bauma, Switzerland

ABOVE LEFT: **Less than one hour from Zürich Airport is Bauma station, which is used by the Dampfbahn-Verein Zürcher Oberland preservation society. On 11 October 2014, steam locomotive 5810 shunts on to its next passenger working.**

ABOVE RIGHT: **Shunting taking place at Bauma ready for the next passenger service with SOB locomotive 196 on 11 October 2014.**

ABOVE LEFT: **One of Europe's most famous locomotives is the Crocodile, which was operated in a number of countries and gauges. A green-liveried example, 13302, stands at Bauma.**

ABOVE RIGHT: **This timber-built hut stands in the locomotive yard at Bauma surrounded by signalling paraphernalia.**

The recently restored BLS Blue Arrow two-car EMU visited Bauma over the weekend of 10/11 October 2014.

ABOVE: *The sides and back of the module illustrated in the previous picture show the simplicity of the layout and its flexibility because different scenic modules can be slotted in at the front.*

LEFT: *Many modellers in Europe seem to prefer to model dioramas and compact layouts rather than tackling a large personal layout. This superb HOm layout measures around 1.2 × 0.6m. To see more excellent modelling, go to www.albulabahn.ch, where there is a video of this module in action.*

An under-construction RhB O-scale layout at the Bauma Show east of Zürich in October 2014. Hard foam sections have been used to form the landscape.

EURO-MODELLING INTERLUDE – WOLPERTINGER HBF

A modern station modelled in N scale as described by Paul Smith.

Wolpertinger Hbf began life as the project layout Singen Hbf in the sadly missed magazine *European Railways* and was the brainchild of Dr Michael Watts. The original concept was for two modules of 1.8 × 0.6m, although in practice the front scenic module is slightly deeper at 690mm and the rear fiddle yard board is 545mm deep. The baseboards and the layout legs are all constructed from 6mm MDF with thinner laminated MDF used to form the curved corners.

The town scene with the main Hauptbahnhof building is above the running lines and platforms and is around 60mm above the baseboard. There is a backscene to the rear and sides of the scenic board, the lower part being made from MDF, with the top part a removable canvas material that can be rolled up for transportation.

As originally built, the layout was wired for cab-control with isolating sections, although this has been altered for Digital Command Control (DCC) operation during the last few years. The complex wiring caused some running issues, so the layout was fitted with Tam Valley Depot's excellent turnout frog power supplies (Hex Frog juicers), which simplified the wiring. DCC operation also allowed for the removal of all isolating sections.

The layout has evolved through the provision of additional storage sidings and an S-Bahn/branch to the rear of the station to permit significant freight operations, with freight services branching off the main line and passing through the rearmost through platform to access the branch line fiddle-yard roads. The S-Bahn services are in the hands of modern BR423 four-car EMUs, with the occasional short-formation (three-coach) push-pull train hauled by either DB BR143 or BR111 electric locomotives. Main-line passenger services are seven- or eight-coach IC rakes in current DBAG Fernverkehr livery with DB 101 or 2 × 218 locomotives and the occasional ÖBB visitor (Österreichische Bundesbahnen – Austrian Federal Railways). Regional services are handled by either push-pull Dopplestock four- and five-car rakes with the latest DB Regio BR146, or single-deck DB Regio stock with BR111 or BR110. Occasionally, a Siemens Desiro DMU provides a change in rolling stock.

Freight services are varied, with a good mix of DB AG, international and private operators. The diesel-hauled services are in the hands of the ubiquitous Class

A good selection of modern German Railways DB rolling stock in N scale.
PAUL SMITH

66/77 (Kato's excellent model in many liveries) and the occasional BR232 Ludmilla, ÖBB Hercules and the latest Voith Gravita from Brawa. Electric-hauled freight features the Bombardier Traxx in its many guises, together with the latest Siemens Vectron and Taurus locomotives. Freight traffic is a mix of traditional mixed freight, with steel and tank wagons featuring, as well as a number of contemporary block trains, including current-day ARS Altmann car carriers and Rocky Rail's superb Arcese piggy-back intermodal wagons.

A nicely modelled locomotive yard and just look at those wires over the turntable!
PAUL SMITH

A good selection of N-scale diesel locomotives stand in the yard at Wolpertinger.
PAUL SMITH

Wolpertinger Hbf on the N-scale layout of Paul Smith. PAUL SMITH

DB Class 423 suburban units cross just outside the station.
PAUL SMITH

WOLPERTINGER HBF LAYOUT PROFILE

Name: Wolpertinger Hbf

Type of layout: continuous three-track main-line run with eight-platform urban station with S-Bahn branch, loco servicing stabling point, including a turntable and hidden storage sidings

Era: Epoch V–VIb

Location: south-eastern Bavaria

Scale: N/1:160

Dimensions: overall dimensions are 1.8 × 1.2m, with operation from the front of layout

Track: Peco Finescale Code 55 (wooden sleeper track and points) and Fleischmann Profi motorized uncoupling ramps and hidden storage sidings

Ballast: Woodland Scenics fine grey ballast. The track and ballast were weathered using Railmatch track dirt and other grey shades using an airbrush

Control: Roco Z21 base station with two smartphones using Roco Z21 software as handsets and Tam Valley Hex Frog juicers to power the turnouts

Locomotives: Brawa, Fleischmann, Kato (Class 66s), Hobbytrain/Lemke and Minitrix

Freight wagons: Brawa, Fleischmann, Hobbytrain, Minitrix and Rocky Rail

Coaching stock: Brawa, Fleischmann and Minitrix

Town scene: various building kits including the Hauptbahnhof from Faller with S-Bahn elements kit-bashed; most of the main town buildings are by Faller home made using floristry

Trees: wire, plaster and Woodland Scenics scatter material, together with other trees by Noch and Busch

Figures: Noch and Preiser

Vehicles: cars and vans by Busch, Herpa and Oxford Diecast. The single-deck bus is by Rietze with the 100+ cars in the multistorey car park sourced cheaply from eBay and repainted with a smaller number of high-quality cars on the top deck and at the front

Scenic materials: Noch and Woodland Scenics

Scenic details: Noch laser-cut plants

Building time: the original baseboards and track were purchased without scenery in 2007, rewired for DCC and the track layout altered during 2008–10. The scenery was completed over the period 2012–14.

CHAPTER THREE

LOCOMOTIVES AND ROLLING STOCK

What locomotives and rolling stock are available?

This chapter will provide a brief overview of the huge selection of model railway equipment that is available for those modelling European lines. For newcomers to European railway modelling, it will give some background knowledge to the huge choice of models from a large number of well-known manufacturers whose products are the most easily obtainable in the UK. It is not possible to include the many smaller manufacturers, simply because the number of manufacturers supplying the European model railway industry is so vast.

The large Mãrklin show layout at the Nuremberg Toy Fair.

HO SCALE

Fleischmann is now part of the same group (Model-leisenbahn) as Roco and Klein Modellbahn, concentrating on classic motive power and N scale, while Roco concentrates more on the modern eras. Fleischmann's HO-gauge and N-gauge Start Sets represent very good value for money, containing a locomotive, wagons or carriages, track, controller and transformer, plus a few accessories. The cost of the set is usually considerably cheaper than the sum total of the components and is perhaps one of the most cost-effective ways to begin European modelling.

The Hornby International brand covers Arnold, Electrotren, Jouef, Lima Expert and Rivarrosi European outline models in N and HO scales. For example, Spanish manufacturer Electrotren retails an HO range, including the Co-Co diesel locomotive in Danish and Spanish state railways liveries, clerestory carriages, Renfe compartment carriages, Talgo carriages, a range of wagons (including Transfesa, Swiss, German, Italian and Danish types), plus accessories including catenary.

Liliput is part of the Bachmann group and produces models in three scales – N standard gauge, HO standard gauge and HOe narrow gauge. Liliput entered the world of N scale several years ago and continues to introduce further additions to the range. Most of the N-scale products announced are ones for which Liliput already make HO-scale models, so they do not need to research anew. A list of Liliput dealers in the UK can be found at www.bachmann.co.uk.

Märklin, LGB, Trix and Minitrix are now part of the Dicky Simba Group, which is a large toy distribution company. Märklin products are still very popular in mainland Europe, using a three-rail 'stud' system rather than the two-rail current collection system used by most other companies. Some locomotives and rolling stock in the Märklin range are available as two-rail Direct Current (DC) models under the Trix brand name. Märklin also produces Gauge 1 ranges.

Piko began in 1949 as a toy manufacturer based in Sonneberg. Its current HO-scale range continues to grow, offering some unusual prototypes including Poland and the Czech Republic. In 2002, the 'Hobby' range was introduced as a range of lower priced locomotives and rolling stock, featuring the all-wheel drive and pick-up, giving good running qualities for a lower price. At the 2006 Nuremberg Toy Fair Piko's first G-scale locomotive was announced (a Taurus electric locomotive) and that range has been subsequently expanded. Piko also has a small range of TT Scale (1:120) locomotives and rolling stock and an N-scale range.

Roco, the Austrian manufacturer, produces an enormous variety of model railway equipment in HO, HOe and TT scales. Its products are based on the prototypes of numerous countries, including

Adding passengers to carriages makes a big visual difference to passenger trains.

Germany, Switzerland, Italy, France, Belgium, Austria, Holland, Sweden, Norway, Greece, Russia, Croatia, Slovenia, Hungary, Finland and Poland. The GeoLine track system is ready ballasted, with the point motors within the ballast so that a hole in the baseboard is not necessary for the electrification of the points. Trams, rail buses, diesel/electric/steam locomotives and rolling stock for the appropriate era are available.

An almost out of the works ÖBB Habbins bogie van seen parked on the Italian side of the Brenner line on 12 July 2012.

A Roco model of the ÖBB Habbins bogie van in HO scale.

In the glass cases at the 2015 Nuremberg Toy Fair Liliput displayed its HO models of Austrian outline trams.

ABOVE: *During 2015, Liliput introduced various colourful versions of the LINT 27 single-car DMU seen here in the showcase at the Nuremberg Toy Fair 2015.*

RIGHT: *There are a huge number of containers carried on Europe's railways. These wagons are by Piko, but ACME, Fleischmann, KombiModell, Roco and others also manufacture container wagons.*

Acme, B-Models, Brawa, ESU, HAG, Jägerndorfer, Gützold, Heljan, Heris, Hobbytrade, Hobbytrain (Mehano), LS Models, NMJ, Rail AD, REE-Modeles, SudExpress and Tillig Bahn are just some of the other European model railway equipment suppliers.

For those who like to use permanent-way vehicles both Kibri and Liliput retail a range of tamping, ballast and track-laying vehicles in HO scale. Kibri also produces a selection of catenary installation rail vehicles plus road vehicles with flashing lights, together with models of the modern Robel track-maintenance vehicle in fully assembled form, some versions of which are motorized in the Viessmann range. Hobbytrain produces motorized versions of the Robel machines in N gauge.

ABOVE: *Rivarossi CIWL Cruising Service Car for use on the Orient Express luxury train. The carriage is numbered 4013 and is the one that David Suchet posed next to whilst making the ITV David Suchet on the Orient Express documentary. The buffers are sprung and there are a lot of already applied parts, such as pipes and handrails. The model comes with several add-on details including piping for the brakes, although these parts can only really be fitted if the model is to be static, because they would be fouled by the coupling if the model was running. There is a lot of nicely applied decals and raised details on the model. One needs a magnifying glass to get the most from looking at the details.*

In October 1883, the first original Orient Express ran from Paris through the Alps, Budapest and Bucharest to Constantinople. This legendary train continued to carry royalty and celebrities between European cities up until its 1920s heyday. After World War II, the increase in popularity of alternatives led to the last service of the Orient Express as a regular passenger train in May 1977. The train was saved by entrepreneur and rail enthusiast, James B. Sherwood. In 1977 he bought two of the train's carriages at a Sotheby's auction in Monte Carlo. Over the next few years, $16 million was spent locating, purchasing and restoring some thirty-five vintage carriages. In May 1982, the famous train was reborn when the Venice Simplon-Orient-Express made its maiden run from London to Venice. Today, the train continues to run as one of the world's most exclusive trains, with many of its carriages restored originals from the 1920s.

OTHER SCALES

LGB was started over 130 years ago and in 1968 announced its first large-size model train in G scale, which led to sales of its products globally.

LGB has been part of Märklin since 2008 and is the best-selling garden railway system worldwide for indoors and outdoors. The company now has over 600 high-quality model railway products in G scale.

RIGHT: A display module by Ferro Train using stock of the Brienz Rothorn Bahn near Lake Brienz in Switzerland. The mountain backscene is particularly convincing. Such a module would be ideal for a space-starved modeller. This scene depicted measures less than 1m by 30cm.

BELOW: O-scale modelling across Europe is gaining momentum, with more and more products for this scale becoming available 'off the shelf'. This layout is based on the Swiss RhB network and appeared at the Bauma 2014 model railway show in Switzerland.

Also within the Märklin model railway empire is its Z-scale range, which was for a long time the smallest scale for ready-to-run products using a scale of 1:220. It enables a layout to be built on a coffee table, a window sill or just a shelf in your bookcase.

N-gauge locomotives and rolling stock are available from Brawa, Kato, Hobbytrade, Jägerndorfer, Lemke, Lima Minitrain (now retailed under the Arnold label),

Mabar, Minitrix, Rocky Rail – these lists, as with all others in this book, are not exhaustive.

Bemo produces superb Swiss metre-gauge HOm (metre-gauge track in 1:87 scale) models of the Rhätische Bahn, Matterhorn Gotthard Bahn, Zentralbahn and Montreux Oberland Bernois locomotives and rolling stock. But they also offer HOe (750mm track in 1:87 scale) products based on German prototypes from Saxony and Wurttemberg.

LEFT: This N-scale layout by David Aldis is vaguely based on the BLS (with its model of the Bietschtal Viaduct), but the rolling stock used is from throughout the country. The rolling stock is whatever takes David's fancy. The layout is located in a loft measuring approximately 5.5 × 3m, with the baseboards being about 60cm wide arranged around the four sides of the loft. Half of the layout has scenery, with the remainder being used for storage sidings. There are two main levels with double-track lines on both, plus a branch line leading up to a third level.

BELOW: The buildings are a mixture of Faller, Vollmer and Pola, with figures by Noch. The road vehicles, including a number of obligatory postbuses, are by Rietze, Wiking and Faller.

RIGHT: *So far, there are 281 trees on the layout, with at least another 200 or more needing to be planted. This N-scale layout does not include catenary at the moment.*

BELOW: *Even in N scale a good level of detailing can be acheived. Landscape foundations are a mixture of hard foam, plaster cloth and cork bark. The scenic materials are mainly Woodland Scenics Fine Turf and Polyfiber, static-grass fibres by Noch and WW Scenics.*

Whilst most are electric and diesel locomotives steam enthusiasts are also catered for. Some Bemo locomotives are fitted for rack operation – these can climb gradients of up to 15 per cent with minimum radii of 40cm. Bemo Start Sets offer very good value for money and provide an ideal introduction to narrow-gauge modelling. The sets are usually based on Swiss prototypes with a locomotive, either passenger or goods stock, and come with a circle of track and one siding.

LEFT: Liliput HOe steam locomotive for use on Austrian narrow-gauge lines.

BELOW: An O-scale model of a Rhätische Bahn Ge 4/4 II 626 'Malans' locomotive.

RIGHT: **Now that Peco has begun to produce HOe (also known as 009) track in sectional pieces it is expected that there will be more interest in this narrow gauge in HO scale. This is the Liliput D11 0-4-0 locomotive based on the Zillertalbahn.**

BELOW: **Swiss narrow-gauge RhB unit 31 halts at the signal on this HOm layout modelled by Stephan Kraus (www.smk-modellbau.de).**

For HOe scale, locomotives and rolling stock are available from a number of companies including Bemo, EggerBahn, Ferrotrain, Halling, Liliput, Mini-trains and Roco.

TT scale still has an active presence in mainland Europe and just some of the companies that cater for it include Tillig offering track, locomotives, rolling stock and accessories, with other manufacturers including JATT, Arnold, Piko, TT Model and more.

The Japanese company of Kato is well known to modellers following the American or Japanese scene, but it is becoming more familiar to European modellers with its N-gauge Eurostar models and various livery models of the SBB Class 460 locomotives. In addition, the company now produces N-scale models of Swiss Glacier Express and RhB Allegra trains to run on N-scale track. While this is not strictly accurate because the trains should be running on Nm track (metre gauge), it shows how popular these trains are.

TT scale is far from dead in Europe. It is in fact very much alive, with a number of big manufacturers supporting it, including Piko, Roco and Tillig.

OPPOSITE PAGE: A large-scale model of the Adler locomotive with Preiser figures.

Products offered by specialist manufacturers supplement the ranges offered by the familiar manufacturers. These include Lematec (in I, IIm, N, Nm, HOm, Om, O and HO scales), HAG, Fulgurex, Lok 14, Philotrain, Bilger and HRF, just to mention a small selection.

The Feldbahn (field railway) system by Busch offers great potential for narrow-gauge modelling following on the heels of its mining railway system. The Hof-scale system uses a track system of 6.5mm rail gauge and two radius of curves plus straights and points. There is a central magnetic strip that runs between the rails that can be disguised by ballast. There are a number of start sets, plus several different wagons.

O-scale models are becoming increasingly popular from Bemo, Brawa, Kiss, Lenz, MTH and others. And in the even larger Gauge 1, an increasing number of products are available from Kiss, KM1 Modellbau and Märklin.

While many of the products from, say, Liliput, Piko and Roco are in their main catalogues, there are some country specials produced solely for retailers of that country. So, for example, the Austrian importer Dolischo, the German company Lemke and Swiss importer Arwico all have special models that are a little challenging to source in the UK. For example, for Swiss retailers BLS Dostos versions of the Liliput Kiss train sets were made available.

An O-scale RhB tractor unit seen at the Bauma model railway show in October 2014.

A SAMPLE OF THE VARIETY OF MOTIVE POWER

To provide the reader with some idea of the scope of European models available I selected Germany and reviewed what models are available for the modern image modeller in the popular scales of the German Railways Class 101 general purpose locomotive (145 prototype locomotives built by Adtranz and introduced from 1996). These are just some of the available models:

- in HO scale by Fleischmann, Märklin, Roco and Trix
- for N gauge Fleischmann and Minitrix
- Märklin produces a Z-gauge model
- and Tillig in TT gauge.

Container traffic is seen throughout mainland Europe. There is a wide range of container wagons produced in both HO and N scales. In addition, container-handling equipment is available from Heljan, with the availability of containers being expanded further by scenic manufacturers offering alternative model containers. HO container-handling equipment is offered by Brawa, Kibri, Vollmer and Roco. Acme, B-Models, Electrotren, Fleischmann, Lilliput, Kombi Model, Liliput, Märklin, Piko, Rivarossi, Roco and Rocky Rail retail container-carrying wagons in HO scale. Kibri, Wiking, Herpa and Albedo manufacture alternative containers. For N scale, Acme, Arnold, B-Models, Fleischmann, Hobbytrain, Minitrix and Rocky Rail retail wagons, with container-handling equipment offered by Brawa and Vollmer.

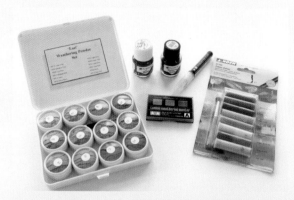 

ABOVE LEFT: **Just a selection of the many weathering products that are available. Weathering is the process of making models look more realistic by simulating the effects of rain, sun, dust, snow, grime and aging. Because relatively few European models are available ready weathered, it is usually up to the purchaser to decide if he wants to weather the models himself. Some of us will understandably choose not to weather our rolling stock because of cost and resale implications, so weathering is very much a personal matter. We can choose how far we want to weather our rolling stock – will it be lightly weathered or very dirty? We can also be selective with our weathering – so, for example, a wagon can be detailed and painted to represent replacement timbers and panels.**

ABOVE RIGHT: **A Roco Railion wagon straight out of the box looks too clean and shiny! The detailing work on the Railion wagon that we discuss here took about an hour, but the result is that I now have a wagon that looks more realistic than the version straight from the box and I gained satisfaction doing the work.**

ABOVE LEFT: **Here are all the add-on bits and pieces that came with this wagon. Many ready-to-run locomotives, wagons and carriages come with a small bag full of detailing parts. Some purchasers choose not to fit these parts to their models; others feel that their model is not complete until they are fitted.**

ABOVE RIGHT: **In this view of the lower wagon side the small holes to take the detailing parts are very obvious.**

continued overleaf

Some of the detailing parts have been added to the wagon and the bogie has been dry-brushed with grey acrylic paint.

Weathering chalks rubbed over the sides of the wagon have highlighted the creases in the cover. The wagon is starting to look a bit more realistic.

ABOVE LEFT: The end of the wagon just as it comes 'out of the box'. It looks far too clean.

ABOVE: The end of the weathered wagon. The dirt and grime effect has settled into the joints so that it looks more like what would be seen on a real wagon.

LEFT: The finished wagon looks very different to the wagon straight 'out of the box'. I intentionally did not weather the information panels on the wagon because these are usually the cleanest part of a wagon in real life.

The SBB Cargo Class 843 diesel Bo-Bo locomotive is used in Switzerland for both shunting and local-run freight services. Here, SBB Cargo locomotive 843 059 stands at Ziegelbrücke station on 1 July 2013.

The Piko HO-scale model of the SBB Cargo Am 843 is good, capturing the overall look of this modern shunting locomotive, but it does need some weathering and the grilles need a little attention.

Here is the same locomotive after the grilles have been highlighted with dark grey paint and yellow warning lines painted on the handrails. These improvements took fifteen minutes, but the locomotive looks a lot more realistic.

CHAPTER FOUR

VALUE FOR MONEY EUROPEAN RAILWAY MODELLING

How to model European railways on a budget.

This book has been slanted towards the beginner rather than those who have already built European layouts. It is my hope that it will encourage a few more enthusiasts of European railways to consider building a European layout or diorama, if only as somewhere to display their models of rolling stock that are currently safely packed away in boxes. Also I hope that modellers who have not looked across the English Channel before as a basis for their layouts may feel inspired to dig a little deeper into the vast choice of European prototypes waiting to be reproduced in miniature.

Whilst some may like the idea of looking across the English Channel for new modelling challenges, many believe that the cost of European outline products is too expensive. It is true that just a few years ago the average retail price of a Bemo, Fleischmann or Roco European locomotive was up to three times that of a British outline Bachmann, Hornby or Lima model, but today the differential is nowhere as great as that. In fact, the gap has closed so much that sometimes equivalent European locomotives that are discounted in the UK might only be 10–20 per cent more expensive than a roughly similar UK locomotive. Some ranges do offer better value for money products than others. For example, Piko retail standard and expert ranges. Some companies such as Jägerndorfer retail standard and premium ('high end') models. Search the advertisements, dealer's shelves, second-hand tables and traders stands at model railway shows for the bargains!

Second-hand items are good value for money and because many European models have generally been acquired as collector's items, they are in mint condition and boxed and are therefore worthwhile purchases. There are some second-hand dealers that advertise in magazines such as *Continental Modeller* and often society magazines include small ads from members wishing to sell some of their models.

This well-stocked model shop is Bahnhof Europa at Gaugemaster (at Ford near Arundel), displaying a wide variety of good-quality European models.

RIGHT: *A compact layout built so that it could catch a glimpse of Austria, France, Germany or Switzerland just by changing the station signage. Catenary still has to be installed.*

BELOW: *Start Sets are a very good way to begin European modelling. The set illustrated here is by the narrow-gauge specialist Bemo and includes an oval of track, a locomotive and five wagons. All that is needed to start running trains is a controller. Many other companies also include a controller and transformer, some of which are DCC Start Sets.*

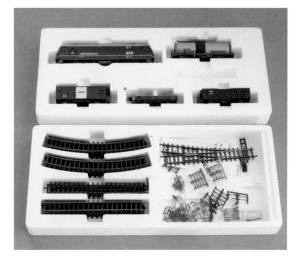

RIGHT: *The contents of one of the Bemo HOm Start Sets. To the lower right can be seen all of the add-on parts for the locomotive and the wagons. Fitting instructions are supplied and Start Sets always work out cheaper to buy than the total cost of the individual contents.*

A small layout may be all that one's pocket will accommodate, but, in my experience, it will be more satisfying to own and operate if it is stocked with good-quality rolling stock that runs beautifully.

Start Sets in both HO and N scales offer excellent value for money, because they usually include a locomotive, rolling stock, track and controller (DC or DCC). Both Fleischmann and Roco retail track packs that can be used to expand upon their Start Sets in stages. Bemo Start Sets in HOm gauge also provide an excellent value for money entry into the narrow-gauge

scene – some sets have passenger stock, while others have freight stock, including a locomotive, rolling stock and an oval of track with a siding.

There are numerous model railway shows in mainland Europe within relatively easy reach of the UK. The annual shows in Utrecht and Cologne are just two (both accessible by Eurostar and connecting train services) and as with other model railway exhibitions 'special show offers' are sometimes available.

A few additional cost-cutting tips may be to buy unpainted people rather than the finished products,

LEFT: *The annual model railway exhibition entitled Ontraxs is held in the railway museum at Utrecht, the Netherlands. The atmosphere at the show is good because the layouts and traders are located within the full-size exhibits.*

BELOW LEFT: *Unpainted figures are a good way to save money when building a layout. The cost of ready-painted HO-scale figures works out at about £1 to £2 per figure. The cost of one unpainted figure from Preiser works out at less than 5p per figure.*

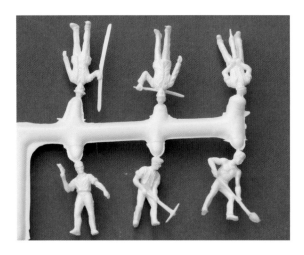

scratch-building your own catenary, buildings and trees, or buying basic models of trees in bulk, then finishing them yourself.

EURO-MODELLING INTERLUDE – HOLZHOF

A compact layout demonstrating what is possible as a first step from a train set.

I have enjoyed building a number of small layouts of various locations in Europe over the past few years and this project is intended to show what is possible

as the next step on from a 'train set', maybe as a first European layout. The aim of this layout was to demonstrate how by just adding a few more pieces of track, a few buildings, a second train and some nice scenery, it is possible to turn a train set into a model railway using products that are readily available from many model shops.

The layout has a continuous run on a single baseboard with potential for running two trains by including a small station with a passing loop and a timber siding and to represent somewhere in Bavaria in the summer months. The scenery was made in the shortest possible time using modern materials, including a Noch laser-cut bridge to cross a wide river. It took five months to build this layout and in total about 120 hours were spent making the layout from the bare baseboard to adding the final details. This time does not include the drying times for the adhesives and paints. I had the baseboard built for me, so the construction time excludes building the baseboard and its legs.

The track is Peco Code 100 Setrack ballasted using Woodland Scenics fine light grey ballast, then weathered using acrylic paints with a light misting from an aerosol can. Alternatively, I could have used Fleischmann Profi or Roco GeoLine track, which is ready ballasted and this would have reduced the building time of the project.

*ABOVE: **A compact HO-scale layout built to show what is possible using 'out of the box' components. The layout called Holzhof measures 1.4 × 1m.***

*RIGHT: **Shunting an Ealos wagon loaded with timber in the loop at Holzhof station. Both the wagon and the DB Class 212 locomotive are by Roco. The use of backscenes makes this layout look a lot bigger than it actually is.***

Railway enthusiasts (HO-scale figures by Noch) look at the Roco DB Class 650 Regio Shuttle, which is framed by the exquisite foliage of a miniNatur spruce tree.

The Stadler DB Class 650 Regio Shuttles by Roco are useful branch passenger trains, being just one carriage in length. The laser-cut bridge kit is by Noch.

The locomotives used on the layout are by Fleischmann, Liliput, Mehano and Roco. I operate the layout in Austrian, French, German and Swiss modes. In German mode, the passenger service is provided by one of the popular Class 650 DB railcars by Roco. The freight services are hauled and shunted by a Fleischmann DB Class 212 locomotive (bought in a Start Set some years ago) and a Roco DB Class 212 locomotive. The wagons are a selection by Electrotren, Fleischmann, Liliput, Mehano, Piko and Roco. I have weathered most of the wagons using a mixture of glass-fibre brush distressing, weathering dyes, aerosol sprays and dry brushing. In some of the open wagons I have added loads of real timber (twigs from the garden).

LANDSCAPE AND SCENICS

Plaster Cloth by Noch and Woodland Scenics was laid over hard foam pieces that were used to form the land contours. Once the plaster cloth had dried, it was painted and then scatter materials were sprinkled on top of some adhesive. Once the glue had dried, static grass fibres of various manufacturers were planted using a Noch Gras-master. Scenic materials came from all the popular names, including Anita Décor, Faller Premium, Heki, miniNatur, Noch and Woodland Scenics.

The rock faces are a mixture of hard foam pieces by Noch (these come ready painted and are very light in weight) and Woodland Scenics Hydrocal pieces that I made in moulds and then painted. The retaining wall was made from Heki flexible embossed stone sheet. The three buildings are two plastic kits (the station building and a timber chalet) by Kibri and a resin platelayers' hut is by Hornby International.

The lineside plants are laser-cut and grass tufts by Noch, with other flowers by miniNatur. Model railway layouts based in the Alps need a lot of trees. This small layout has over 125 trees, mainly of coniferous types. They came from a variety of companies, including Anita Décor, Bachmann Scene Scapes, Busch, Faller, Gaugemaster, Heki, Noch and Woodland Scenics. I decided to buy some miniNatur trees for this layout and am very pleased with them – they look superb.

I made the river bed and the river banks using sections of hard foam cut with a Woodland Scenics Foam Knife. The hard foam used was sections of loft insulation and leftover pieces of Woodland Scenics Risers that I had to hand. The hard foam sections were covered with plaster-impregnated cloth. Woodland Scenics Realistic Water was used to represent the water in the river. In the central area of the river it was simply a matter of pouring it straight from the plastic bottle and letting it find its own level. Along the edges of the river I used a plastic syringe to provide a controlled amount of fluid so that it did not run 'up' the river bank. The bridge kit used on the layout is one of the range of Noch laser-cut bridge kits.

IS BUYING A START SET A GOOD INTRODUCTION?

Buying a Start Set is a very good way to begin European railway modelling, because they usually contain sufficient parts to get a train running within a short time after opening the box. All the component parts of a Start Set can be used on future layouts as one moves on in the hobby. They are generally very competitively priced – the package usually costs less than the sum of the parts. Normally, a train set includes a locomotive, several wagons or carriages, an oval of track, a controller/transformer and the necessary connections from the track to the controller. At the time of writing, Roco, for example, produces HO-scale DCC Start Sets that are available at UK dealers for around £250, including a full DCC system.

The importance of train sets to the hobby is that they are used as bait to attract more active modellers. A train set on its own might not contain enough 'goodies' to firmly establish someone in the hobby, but by buying an additional item or two the owner of a train set will realize that there is a lot more to railway modeling than simply running trains around an oval of track.

So when buying a Start Set as a present for someone, or indeed for oneself, if the budget allows another purchase or two at the same time this might prove worthwhile. Other purchases might include: a track pack to improve the variety of the train movements; two carriages, if, for example, the train set includes wagons and a building kit; or a scenery starter kit. These will all expand on the 'play value' and interest factor of a train set at a comparatively low additional cost.

ABOVE LEFT: *DB Class 212 169 loco by Roco crosses a laser-cut card bridge by Noch. The weathering of the wagon is described in this chapter.*

ABOVE RIGHT: *Small trackside details such as these identify a specific country of operation. This distance post of Germany is one of a detailing pack by Noch in HO scale.*

RIGHT: *The Fleischmann loco and wagons were part of a Start Set purchased over twenty years ago. The building is a kit by Kibri that is also twenty years old.*

CONCLUSION

Because I have such varied European railway interests (I like the railways of Austria, France, Germany and Switzerland and lots more!) from time to time I change the signs and the rolling stock on the layout so that it can become an Austrian, French, German or a Swiss layout. This layout has been really good to run trains on because it is stored in my garage but takes me only five minutes to position it on its legs, to plug in the controller and the trains are running! It has been reliable to operate and the track does not take much time to keep clean.

Holzhof was fun to build and I am pleased how it has turned out. I hope that I have captured a little of the look of the Alps in Central England and maybe this layout has given you some ideas on how to build a simple but attractive layout as somewhere to run your European locomotives and rolling stock.

HOLZHOF LAYOUT PROFILE

Name:	Holzhof
Type of layout:	compact continuous run with a small station
Era:	Epoch V
Location:	somewhere in the Alps
Scale:	HO
Dimensions:	1.51 × 1.08m (on one baseboard)
Track:	Peco Code 100 Setrack
Ballast:	Woodland Scenics fine light grey ballast; the track and ballast were weathered using acrylic paints
Control:	Gaugemaster Combi DC analogue
Locomotives and diesel units:	Brawa, Fleischmann, Liliput, Mehano and Roco
Freight wagons:	Electrotren, Liliput, Mehano, Piko and Roco
Landscaping:	Woodland Scenics Plaster Cloth laid over hard foam pieces; the plaster cloth was then painted and treated with scatter materials and later with static grass fibres of various manufacturers using a Noch Gras-master.
Rock faces:	Noch hard foam and Woodland Scenics Hydrocal pieces
Retaining wall:	Heki flexible embossed stone sheet
Buildings:	Kibri and Hornby International
Trees:	Anita Décor, Bachmann Scene Scapes, Busch, Heki and miniNatur
Figures:	Noch and Preiser
Scenic materials:	Anita Décor, Faller Premium, Heki, miniNatur, Noch and Woodland Scenics
Scenic details:	Noch and Walthers laser-cut plants
Fencing:	Duha, Faller and Noch
Building time:	120 hours over five months.

CHAPTER FIVE

CATENARY SYSTEMS

What are the options for modellers wanting to add catenary to a layout?

Catenary is used throughout most of Europe and is arguably needed for many European railway layouts. It is the one thing many of us cannot get out of doing if we want to make our layouts look realistic, but erecting catenary can be a new modelling challenge for many. There are several aspects of building the catenary that a modeller might worry about, including will the masts be in the right place? Will they be vertical? Will the wires meet and will the pantographs touch the wires?

After experimenting with numerous systems, I now find that adding the catenary to a layout is one of the most satisfying aspects of modelling European railways. 'Putting up the wires' makes a huge visual difference to any layout, immediately transforming it into something more European by allowing both diesel and electric traction to be run legitimately side by side.

There are a number of companies that make catenary systems for the popular scales, including Hobbex, Hornby International, JV, Sommerfeldt and Viessmann. Those who do not wish to use proprietary products can scratch-build their own systems using aircraft control wire, for example. Masts can be formed from the model H girders and similar that are retailed in both plastic and metal.

One possible shortcut in erecting a catenary system is not to install the wires. Some modellers in mainland Europe are content just to have masts on their layouts, but this will not satisfy many modellers

Alpmitholz layout used with Viessmann catenary, which is very much a 'clip-fit' system that can be erected in the minimum of time.
CHRIS NEVARD/MODEL RAIL

that trouble-free running is possible with pantographs in the raised position. But there are ways around this that look better, which we will cover later.

Do not let studying the real thing put you off putting up some masts on your own layout, because even a relatively basic catenary system in model form can look good. It will certainly look better than no catenary at all.

HOW TO INSTALL CATENARY

STUDY THE PROTOTYPE

Before attempting to install catenary in model form go out and look at the equipment and the construction techniques used on the prototype. Stand by a stretch of line that has overhead lines (OHL) and look at the masts, the wires and the equipment that is necessary to keep the wires in place. There is a lot more to it than may be first imagined.

Look at pictures of electrified lines in magazines, books and your own photographs. You will be surprised by how much you will learn. Catenary is something we take for granted until we need to add it to our own layout.

and it is, of course, best to see both the masts and the wires in place. That said, in the smaller scales such as N and Z installing wires is not so crucial. One simple way to add a basic wire is to use elastic thread between the arms of the masts. This gives some form of a 'wire' linking the masts, even if it is a basic representation.

Some layout operators run their locomotives with the pantograph down, maybe because the operator does not have sufficient confidence

*TOP LEFT: **There is a fairly comprehensive catenary system for followers of Austrian, German or French railways made by Hobbex. There are various types of mast for HO scale – lattice, round, solid and H profile. The masts are plastic, which makes them light in weight and flexible enough to take the odd unintentional knock. For N scale, the range is a lot smaller. Both for HO and N scale there are sets available with a variety of components.***

*LEFT: **There is no getting away from it, most lines in Europe need catenary. This picture was taken at Biberbrugg in central Switzerland.***

LEARNING ABOUT MODELLING CATENARY

Read other modellers' accounts of building their catenary in magazines and books, because different techniques can be learnt and tips gained. Type something like 'modelling catenary' or 'HO catenary' into an Internet search engine and you will soon gain access to a wealth of information. There are some YouTube videos demonstrating how to assemble catenary systems.

The Sommerfeldt catalogue and wiring guide are both useful background reading. They will help to clarify terms such as 'messenger wire' and 'radius pull-off'. Both booklets contain text in English and even if you choose not to use the Sommerfeldt products, reading these publications will provide information about the general principles of catenary.

Where exhibition layouts feature catenary, take the opportunity to chat to the operators and they will usually be ready to pass on their experiences.

PLANNING FOR CATENARY

It is best to consider the installation of the catenary at the planning stage of a new layout. If an open-plan framework baseboard is to be used, thought must be given to where the masts will go. Some masts carry a screw thread that needs to go through the baseboard, with a nut attached to it underneath the baseboard; one such system is Sommerfeldt. Others fix the masts on top of the baseboard, including Hobbex, Hornby International and Viessmann. It is important that the track bed timber is wide enough to take the track and an additional margin for the catenary mast.

Give consideration to the material to be used for the baseboard, because if it is too soft (such as insulation board, polystyrene or hard foam), it may not be possible to fix the masts firmly enough. Weather and ballast the track before installing the catenary, because it will be very difficult to do this after the wires and masts are in place.

ERECTING THE CATENARY

Give yourself a dry run with a few masts and wires before you drill any holes. Play around with the bits and pieces of the system to improve your confidence as you start to build the overhead system. Erect just a handful of masts at a time and test them fully with the contact wires and passing trains before moving on to the next section.

A Sommerfeldt display diorama showing HO-scale catenary for German Railways (DB).

Double-check that each mast will not be struck by the longest carriages or locomotives that will be used on the layout. The sharper the track radius, the closer the masts will be to each other and the shorter the contact wires will be.

On a straight section of track the overhead wire should run in a slight zigzag. In real life, this prevents constant wear on one section of the pantograph. Bear in mind the general principle, which is that the wire should be located somewhere near to the centre of the space between the rails.

Ideally, choose the thinnest contact wires that you can find to give maximum realism. Some companies such as Sommerfeldt retail a choice of 'standard' and 'finer' gauge contact wires.

Most modellers choose not to erect catenary in hidden storage sidings by providing a transition section, which may be a curved section of rail soldered on to the last wire so that the pantograph moves up and down on it.

Depending upon the method of catenary construction, care needs to be given to the underside of the wire if you intend to run the pantographs under the wire. One area that can cause problems is excessive solder at joints, which can create a bumpy underside of the wire. A small file will usually remedy this. Some systems just require the wires to be clipped together (such as the Viessmann system), so solder will not be needed.

Some modellers paint the contact wires, while others leave them in their plain form. Shiny metal does not always look too realistic in my eyes, but this is a matter of personal choice. Spray-painting contact wires a relatively dark colour makes them less visually obvious and it is definitely best to paint the wires before they are positioned on the masts.

Putting up the wires on a straight stretch of track is quite easy, because the lengths of the wire can be relatively long. On curves, it becomes more challenging, as the masts need to be positioned more closely

A track maintenance team stands beneath a Sommerfeldt catenary system on a Heki display diorama.

together and the wires are shorter. It is important that the wire is fixed in the correct position in relation to the pantograph of a locomotive, because if the wire is too high the pantograph will not reach the wire. If it is too low, the pantograph will push too much on the wire, which will look unrealistic and not provide smooth operation of the trains; if the wire is too far from the centre line, the pantograph will slip off the wire – either inside or outside the wire.

Finally, building the catenary is something that should be enjoyed and not be rushed.

PANTOGRAPHS THAT DO NOT TOUCH THE WIRES

Where the pantographs are not raised on moving trains, much of the realism of a layout with fitted catenary is lost. Understandably, a modeller might be concerned about the damage that a rogue pantograph may bring, but there are a couple of easy ways to run pantographs in the upright position that do not touch the wires. One method is to position the pantograph just below the wires using cotton or thin wire to hold it just below the lowest point of the wires.

Alternatively, using something like an open staple you can push one part of the 'clip' beneath part of the lower pantograph structure on the roof of the locomotive, with the other end clipped in below the top part of the pantograph. Each pantograph is slightly different, so it is a matter of looking at each individual locomotive to see how this is possible. Then fold over the staple using fine pliers to make it as discreet as possible. By using either of these methods, from normal viewing distances it will not be too obvious that the pantograph is not touching the wire.

MATERIALS AND TOOLS FOR ERECTING CATENARY

The minimum materials and tools required for catenary installation are an electric mini-drill for making the holes in the baseboard to take the masts where a long fixing thread is required, a pencil for marking the position of the masts, a ruler for measuring the space between the masts, a small pair of pliers for bending the wires over the mast arms, and a fine-tipped soldering iron and solder if you choose to solder the wires. Good eyes or a pair of glasses to notice if the mast is not upright are useful!

Paintbrushes can be used for highlighting the details, such as the insulators, and a small screwdriver for fixing the masts to the baseboard. Dark brown or dark grey acrylic aerosols or airbrush paint can be used to colour the wires, though some modellers leave the wires as they come.

Take the longest item of rolling stock that you will use on the layout to test that the posts cannot be struck by a passing train.

When a line leaves the scenic part of a layout and no wires are erected in the storage yard, the pantograph needs to be moved up or down from the wire. One way of doing this is to use brass wire, as has been done here by Stephan Kraus. STEPHAN KRAUS

Double-track section of electrified track on a Heki display using Sommerfeldt catenary, showing a catenary supply station in the background.

USING THE VIESSMANN SYSTEM

It is claimed that this catenary system is one of the simplest on the market today. It does not require any soldering and one simply clips the pieces in place. For HO scale, lengths of contact wire are available ranging from 140mm to 400mm. In addition, the company produces a selection of wires for specific track components for various European track systems. Some wires are called 'Universal', indicating that the ends of the wires are not pre-bent for clipping over the catenary mast. Other wires are available ready bent on both wires at each end.

Viessmann recommends that a mast should be used every 22.5 degrees of curve and its masts arrive with a 'foot' that includes small grooves across

it. These grooves show the correct distance that the mast is to be positioned in relation to the track. The instruction leaflet enclosed with the Start Set says which groove is appropriate to which track system. The foot of the mast needs to be tight up against the track sleepers. For Peco OO/HO track, for example, it is suggested that the 'Fleischmann Gleis' (track) marking is used. If you are using foam ballast strip, all the grooves of the foot need to be cut off to accommodate the foam.

The catenary system can be used either as a non-working system, or to power a locomotive through the wires and pantograph. To electrify the system it is necessary to use Power Mast (4111) and a Fuse (4188), with a Power Mast being installed roughly every 3m to maintain a good power supply.

On this double-track section of track, German-style Viessmann catenary masts and wires have been used 'straight out of the box'. This catenary system is one of the simplest to use.

Side view of the Viessmann foot on the catenary post – the grooves show where the base is to be cut off for different track systems. Cleverly, the base of the Viessmann masts have a hidden hole for the supplied screw to fix it to the baseboard.

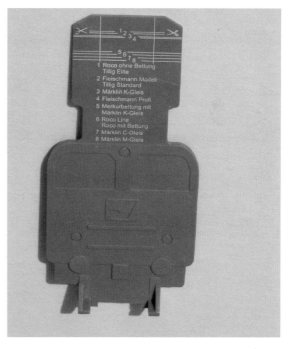

The Viessmann tool supplied with its Start Sets to enable the wires and masts to be erected in the correct position relative to the track.

The base and foot of a Viessmann catenary mast showing the movement that is possible to get the mast in the correct place in relation to the wires and track using this system. The 'grooves' section of the foot were cut off to accommodate the foam underlay used on this layout.

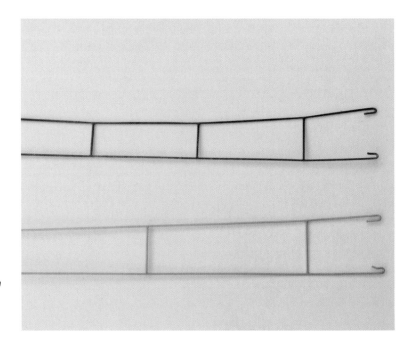

The Viessmann standard wires shown as they come in the bottom part of the picture, then after being sprayed with dark brown acrylic paint at the top.

Parts are available to build wire tensioners and other detail aspects of catenary equipment. The current supply wire (contact wire) and support wires can be purchased ready assembled, but if you wish to use finer section wire it may be necessary to build your own.

This Viessmann catenary system does what it says on the box (though sadly the written instructions are in German). It is simple to use and enables catenary to be erected quickly and the overall good appearance of this catenary has a lot going for it and is especially recommended for 'first-time' catenary builders.

For more information, the company's website is www.viessmann-modell.de. The product is available from several UK retailers, including A&H Models, Gaugemaster and Golden Valley Hobbies.

To demonstrate erecting a basic catenary system we will use a Viessmann Start Set, which is available for N and HO scales. The masts supplied in the Start Sets are German in outline, though other masts are available. In both scales, Viessmann produces Start Sets that can be easily extended with a wide range of individual masts, wires and so on. The OO/HO Start Set (stock number 4100) has sufficient parts for a small oval of single track, including fourteen masts (part 4110), twelve wires (4142) and two longer wires (4143).

INSTALLING THE MASTS

The step by step process to erect the catenary is to use a pencil to mark the baseboard where the screw hole for the foot of the mast is to go. All Viessmann masts screw into the baseboard and the hole will take the supplied screw. The mast and the foot slide together, with the foot being attached to the baseboard first, then the mast sliding into it. Drill a small hole into the baseboard of the correct size for the screw that is supplied with the mast.

Screw the foot securely on to the baseboard, then slide the mast into the foot. Check that the mast is positioned vertically, at 90 degrees to the track, and is positioned correctly to carry the wire centrally over the track. Make any adjustments either by loosening the screw and changing the angle of the mast, or by sliding the mast forwards or back in the foot. There is a little adjustment possible around the hole in the foot of the mast.

FITTING THE WIRES

Enclosed with the Starter Set is a blue plastic Height Positioner for use with the catenary wires. The masts need to be fixed to the baseboard at the correct intervals of the chosen fixed-length wires. To check this distance between the masts lie the wire on the track and mark the centre point of the two bent ends of each wire just outside the ballast.

To fix the wires on to the masts gently push the bent ends of the wires over the arms of the mast – the top and bottom ones. The arms on the masts have a grey plastic covering that holds the wires quite tightly. Do the same on the next mast, leaving the first wire in place. Work along to the next wire and fix it to the masts in the same way. When you are happy that the masts are at 90 degrees to the track, that the wires lie centrally over the track and that there is no excessive pull or stretch in the wires, use a pair of small pliers to tighten the bent ends of the wires over the arms.

OTHER SYSTEMS

HOBBEX

This is a comprehensive system for followers of Austrian, French or German railways with four types of mast – lattice, round, solid and H profile. The masts are plastic, which makes them light in weight and flexible, so able to take the odd unintentional knock. The masts are available with long or short arms. In addition to masts, there are towers with cross-span hangers, tension assemblies, isolators and other component parts available. Wires are sold in three lengths: 354mm, 177mm and 150mm, which can be reduced in length if necessary.

The above information applies to the HO-scale catenary system. For N scale, the Hobbex range is a lot smaller. Both for HO and N scale there are sets available with a variety of components. In the UK the retailer is Winco, which offers a mail-order service and is present at some model railway shows (www.winco.uk.com).

HORNBY INTERNATIONAL

Hornby International produces catenary components in HO scale, including composite wires of differing lengths and a choice of masts (for German or Spanish railways). The posts are in concrete, lattice and high-speed styles, with some of the masts suitable for tramways. Power masts are available so that the wires can be electrified. These are available in the UK and the prices are competitive.

SOMMERFELDT

Sommerfeldt manufactures an extensive range of catenary parts for N, HO, HOm, Om, TT and O scales. These parts include German (DB), Italian (FS), French (SNCF), Belgian (SNCB), Swiss (SBB and narrow-gauge private companies) and Austrian (ÖBB) catenary systems. In addition to overhead systems, the company also manufactures pantographs. To get the best out of this system it is necessary to be relatively skilled with a fine-pointed soldering iron, although some modellers have found that the parts can be assembled using superglue. Their website is www. sommerfeldt.de. In the UK, the products are available from Winco and other retailers.

VARIOUS OTHER COMPANIES

Other manufacturers retailing catenary parts include JV and Ferro Suisse in HO scale and Vollmer for N gauge. Microscale (www.microscale.ch) produces very good quality catenary systems for Swiss-based railways. Kato produces a catenary system for its Unitrack systems in N scale (www.katomodels.com/index_e.shtml).

Noch produces a pack with the parts for a catenary system in which a Helix is used on a layout in all the common scales (www.noch.com). Märklin manufacturer catenary systems in various scales, including Z and HO scales (www.maerklin.com).

Another view of the loop on the author's HO-scale layout, with a Roco SBB Class 460 in Tilsiter cheese livery unusually pulling just one loaded Eaos wagon. The catenary is by Viessmann, with wires that were sprayed dark brown with a Humbrol acrylic aerosol. CHRIS NEVARD/MODEL RAIL

CHAPTER SIX

TRACK

What are the track options for those building European layouts?

In addition to the familiar 'ready to run' standard-gauge track systems available in the UK, there are various other European manufacturers offering comprehensive ranges of track, including Fleischmann, Märklin, Piko, Roco and Tillig. With the variety of European track systems it is not always easy to use sectional pieces of track from different manufacturers interchangeably because rail heights differ and fishplates differ; some systems are ready ballasted, others are not. It is therefore important to do research before purchasing track.

Those who are setting out on a first layout may prefer the simplicity of the sectional track systems, but if it is realism that you want finer-scale flexible track is the preferred way forwards. Flexible track can be mixed with sectional track where the track is of the same Code (the height of the rail) by the same

company. Most sectional track pieces come complete with fitted rail joiners (fishplates), so this is certainly a quick way to start laying track. Sectional track ranges include such accessories as level crossings, inspection pits, buffer stops, uncoupling units, power connecting clips, track pins and foam ballast inlays for plain track and points.

Some of the Start Sets from the main manufacturers come complete with some track – this is usually an oval of track, with or without a siding. The track supplied with the train sets can be expanded by track packs (a specific number of pieces that might, for example, add a loop or a siding to the train set), or by adding any number of additional track pieces from the manufacturers' ranges.

Narrow-gauge modellers are also well catered for with Bemo, Peco, Shinohara and Tillig producing metre-gauge track for HO scale, which is suitable for most Swiss narrow-gauge trains. Peco's 12mm HOm track range includes flexible track, straight and curved points, crossings, buffers and turntables. HOe track (also known as 009) is suitable for many Austrian and German narrow-gauge systems. The Peco HOe track system has recently been expanded to include sectional pieces, which will make track-laying in this popular gauge much easier for beginners.

Which scale do you choose? There is a lot of choice if you model European railways. To the left is HOm narrow gauge, to the centre HO standard gauge and to the right is HOe narrow gauge.

STANDARD GAUGE

Fleischmann's Profi track is very reliable in my experience and is well built, with their ready-ballasted track (Profi Gleis) available in both HO and N scales incorporating wood-coloured sleepers with a ballast surround. The rails are of nickel silver and their advertising literature explains: 'it is strong enough to withstand being walked on'. It is also available in track packs and as separate components, including points, sectional and flexible track, uncoupling ramps, rack, buffers, level crossings and so on. The point motors fit alongside the turnouts, alleviating the need to make holes in the baseboard. The points are sold in 'live' mode, but by simply removing the wire clips between the rails the point is converted into isolating mode. I have found the track to be robust, simple and fast to lay and hard-wearing. The Fleischmann HO track range features a superb turntable that can be extended to forty-eight roads!

Kato Unitrack system for both N and HO scales was initially introduced for the Japanese market, where domestic space is at a premium and permanent layouts are a rarity. So the track was designed to withstand repeated set up and break down of layouts. The Kato retail M (Master) and V (Variation) Unitrack sets allow a purchaser to expand their layouts. Unitrack can be useful for a beginner because of its 'clip-fit' ability and good range of geometry. Unitrack uses UniJoiners, which are simple to fit. The track is pre-ballasted and raised, allowing point motors to be fitted under the trackwork as standard to all turnouts. There are also numerous additional items such as bridges and incline piers, buildings and so on. To my

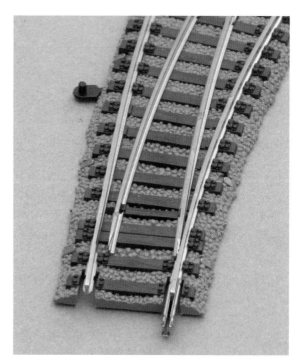

Close-up of Fleischmann Profi ready-ballasted point, which I have found to be reliable, if a little noisy, in use.

eyes, the N-scale system looks a little more realistic than the HO-scale system.

The HO range of Märklin uses a third-rail track system. This system is a lot more popular in mainland Europe than in the UK and whilst the central stud has become more discreet over the years, it does limit the rolling stock that you can use on a layout. Some of the larger manufacturers such as Liliput and Roco do retail third-rail rolling stock for Alternating Current (AC) systems, but they are not produced in such numbers as those for DC (two-rail) systems. Locomotives pick up the electrical current from small stud contacts located in the centre of the sleepers. Märklin advertising literature claims that 'this third "rail" eliminates polarity problems in wiring, and ensures reliable electrical pickup from the track to the locomotive'. Märklin introduced Z gauge (1:220 scale) in 1972 (www.guidetozscale.com/html/catenary.html).

Peco manufactures track for gauges 1, G-45, SM-32, O, HO, HOm, HOe, N and Z. Some have

Ready-ballasted track is available in both N and HO scale. The top two pieces are HO-scale Roco track (GeoLine and RocoLine track) with Fleischmann Profi track at the bottom of the picture.

wooden sleepers with others featuring concrete and steel sleepers. The Setrack sectional pieces come in a range of geometry supplemented by flexible track. The HO Setrack is a Universal Code 100 rigid-unit track system with wooden sleepers and Code 100 nickel silver rail that can be combined with Peco Code 100 flexible track, which can be shaped to form gentle curves or simply to produce a long straight without the need to put several sections of Setrack together.

The Peco Code 75 ('fine' scale) flexible track system has live frog points (Electrofrog) with a similar range to the Code 100 insulated range of points. Most of the rolling stock from the current ranges in HO scale should run on Code 75 track without any problems because wheel flanges are much finer than they were in the past. If you do have any older items of rolling stock that you wish to run on Code 75 track it is generally quite a simple task to re-wheel the item of stock using modern metal axles from the manufacturers. Live frog points may offer better current collection for locomotives, but in my recent experience most modern locomotives run superbly over insulated points because of multiple-wheel current collection. There is a Peco product (SL-112) called Combined Rail Joiners that joins code 75 and Code 100 rails for HO scale.

Piko has a good range of sectional and flexible track in HO scale, plus Code 332 G-scale track using

brass rails with sleepers made from high-density polyethylene that are suitable for use outdoors, being compatible with most other brands of G-scale track, including LGB and AristoCraft.

Roco's wide range of ready-ballasted HO Roco-Line track has been superseded by its GeoLine range, which also usefully conceals the point motors in the grey ballast base. Sectional and flexible track are available, with a choice of points and crossings in Code 83.

Tillig's Elite track system has a height profile of 2.07mm with Code 83 rail. The track is sold both as flexible and sectional components, with a good variety of geometry options – there are four different radii of sectional track curves. The rails come ready aged, with one-piece machined blades. The 950mm lengths of flexible track are retailed with wooden, steel or concrete sleepers. There is a good range of points, crossings and slip points and some of the HO standard-gauge track pieces are sold with integrated

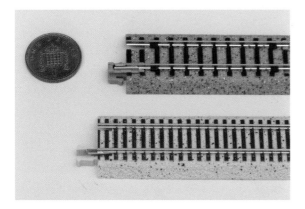

At the top is ready-ballasted track for N scale by Kato. Atlas makes the track at the bottom of the picture that incorporates US sleeper spacing.

Tillig has a good range of realistic ballast inserts for its HO-scale track range.

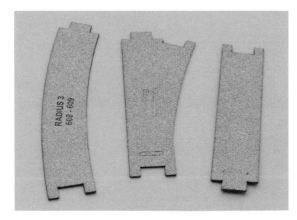

Proses makes ready-shaped cork ballast for points that are useful for sound-deadening.

Proses produces a number of helix for model railways in N and HO scales and in the UK these are available from Golden Valley Hobbies.

sections of narrow-gauge (in both HOm and HOe) track, including points, plain track and crossings. The track range includes some accessories such as platforms, level crossings and so on. The Tillig Elite catalogue is thoroughly recommended for those wishing to use Tillig track, because it is available in English and it contains a useful explanation, in words and pictures, on how to use the Styrostone ballasting system and the various dual-track system pieces.

Weinert (www.weinert-bauteile.de) makes very well-detailed HO track. Proses and other companies produce a helix system for both HO and N scales.

NARROW GAUGE

The two most popular European narrow-gauge railway systems are HOe and HOm. The former is compatible with 009 and will be suitable for Austrian and German systems, whereas HOm is metre gauge in HO scale suitable for lines in France, Germany and mainly Switzerland. Hartel and Kato retail track for trams.

Narrow-gauge modellers are increasingly well catered for by manufacturers. For example, metre-gauge track for HO scale (known as HOm) is available from Bemo, Shinohara and Peco. The Peco 12mm HOm track range (Code 75) includes flexible track, straight and curved points, crossings, buffers and turntables. Peco HOe track (Code 80) is now available in both Setrack and flexible format.

The Bemo HOm range includes set straight and curved track, flexible lengths, curved and straight points, crossovers and double slips, rack track, point motors and Styroplast ballast pieces. Other useful

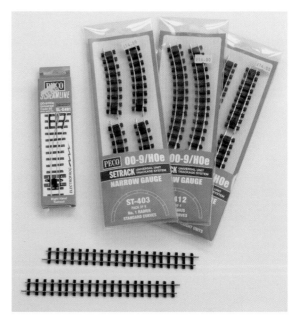

HOe track – more commonly known as 009 track in the UK – is now available in sectional pieces by Peco. This will be very useful for models of many of Austria's narrow-gauge lines that use 760mm-gauge track.

This superb brick factory scene is based on the Busch Feldbahn Hof-scale system, which uses a track system of 6.5mm rail gauge and two radii of curves, plus straights and points. There is a central magnetic strip that runs between the rails, which can be disguised by ballast. BUSCH/GOLDEN VALLEY HOBBIES

parts are a plastic rerailer, signals, buffer stops, corrugated huts and track-plan books. Bemo's range of HOe track is smaller.

The Feldbahn (field railway) system by Busch is an HOf scale system that uses a track system of 6.5mm rail gauge and two radii of curves, plus straights and

points. There is a central magnetic strip that runs centrally between the rails, which can be disguised by ballast. The company is expanding the system and the rolling stock each year.

As with all model railway layouts, it is best to use the largest radius curves that space permits. Sharp curves will not look as out of place on a narrow-gauge mountain line as they will on a high-speed standard-gauge line.

One of the major trends in current railway modelling in Europe is the expansion of digital control. This topic is outside the scope of this book, but it is recommended that manufacturers' catalogues be studied if one is interested in this growing facet of the hobby. There is a lot of choice out there! Manufactured control systems are being developed quickly and it is worth doing one's homework on this subject before purchasing any equipment.

EURO-MODELLING INTERLUDE – KAPRUN AND MORE

A scenic Austrian narrow-gauge layout by John Atkinson.

John models the Austrian and German scenes in both HOe and N scales. His long-term project is building a representative N-gauge model based on the Regensburg (Bavaria, Germany) area that he operates with a detailed timetable closely following the actual service pattern. He also has an exhibition HOe layout – Kaprun (SLB) – based on the well-known Pinzgauer Lokalbahn narrow-gauge line in Land Salzburg, Austria. John takes full advantage of budget airlines and Eurostar to make short trips to Europe to see the prototype first hand.

John chooses to model European railways because there is a vast and varied array of prototypes to choose from and, despite the growing use of multiple-unit trains, there are still plenty of loco-hauled trains and much freight traffic. In many places, cross-border traffic provides further prototype variety, as does the considerable number of Open Access Operators, providing both passenger and freight services.

Information is readily available from specialist societies and publications and researching the prototype is relatively easy and cheap, and can be great fun. There is a great choice of available high-quality models in several scales and eras from the leading proprietary manufacturers. Out-of-the-box detail on

the models is generally far higher than is traditional in the UK and Start Sets provide an easy and economical way into the hobby for beginners.

HOME LAYOUT IN N SCALE

The same layout takes less space than in larger scales and a more complex layout is achievable in the same space, with greater scenic development possibilities. Longer runs of 'open track' are feasible and look more like the prototype. Prototypical-length main-line passenger and goods trains are more practicable. Eight- or nine-coach trains can, with some thought, be accommodated in relatively modest areas and the models are of such good quality that they can be run at speed in push–pull mode without fear of derailing.

These features combine to enable John to operate Regensburg Süd with a junction station on an international main line, a high-level secondary main line, two branches and an open country stretch, all in a space that would only permit a modest HO layout. There is an excellent choice of available models, particularly for the Germanic countries. The choice has widened greatly in recent years and modern technology has made modelling even the less prominent countries feasible with a little research and effort.

HOe EXHIBITION LAYOUT

There remain in Austria a few – and in Switzerland far more – narrow-gauge lines operating in similar manner to standard-gauge lines, that is, as 'proper railways', not just preserved, seasonal enthusiasts' museum pieces. Some of the prototypes are as large as standard-gauge motive power and rolling stock, but the narrow track facilitates reaching more difficult and scenically attractive locations.

Austria was unusual in that many narrow-gauge lines were built to a common 760mm gauge and this was adopted throughout the pre-World War I Austro-Hungarian Empire. There has been much interchange of stock between lines, both within Austria and to/from the Czech Republic, Slovakia, Hungary and the Balkan countries. So there is plenty of rolling stock variety to be modelled.

ABOVE: **John Atkinson's HOe-scale model of Kaprun is a very good representation of Austrian narrow gauge.**
CONTINENTAL MODELLER

BELOW: **The track on the Kaprun layout is HOe gauge. This track is now available in sectional pieces from Peco.**
CONTINENTAL MODELLER

The tall backscene on Kaprun adds to the feeling of depth on the layout based on narrow-gauge railways of Austria. CONTINENTAL MODELLER

The extensive variety of HO-scale scenic accessories and road vehicles can be readily drawn upon when constructing HOe layouts. Though a great many are of German prototypes, Austria and Switzerland and to a lesser extent Italy are reasonably catered for and the search for that 'special item' can be rewarding.

It is not coincidental that John also enjoys visiting Austria's beautiful mountains and valleys on 'research trips'!

OPERATING A EUROPEAN LAYOUT SUCCESSFULLY

Many modellers, often with excellent technical skills, are undoubtedly more interested in constructing their models or layouts than in actually operating them. Their exquisite locomotives, rolling stock, buildings or scenic work can be an inspiration to us all and help to raise our standards. That said, certainly for many of us, actually running the trains is what it's all about and this can be done in many ways.

A lot of satisfaction can be derived from simply watching any train you fancy working its way along or around the layout – and that's fine. However, the 'train set' approach does not suit everyone and many modellers seek to emulate the prototype more closely. This is particularly so where a real-life location forms the subject of a layout, but also for the perhaps larger number of modellers who seek to design and operate a layout representative of a certain prototype style – for example, an Austrian Alpine branch line, or a French coastal main line.

In both cases, the key phrase is 'operating a credible service', which means that the operation of the trains reflects those that run or ran at the chosen real or imagined location. This can initially appear daunting, especially when modelling European railways, but need not be so as plenty of help is at hand. The necessary information can be obtained from several sources, of which published books, magazine articles and DVDs are very important. Photographs in particular assist in ensuring that modellers can operate appropriate train formations.

Fortunately, there are several publishers of English-language materials on European railways, but you will also usually find local publications helpful. Even without knowledge of the relevant language, the photographs can be readily understood and it is amazing how quickly one picks up enough technical terms to understand the captions. Membership of relevant specialist societies also yields much information. Sooner or later, however, some personal research will prove beneficial and this can be simply achieved.

A good starting point is to obtain the passenger timetable for the location you are seeking to model (or visit the relevant website). This is naturally simplest where you are modelling contemporary practice in a real location. In recent years, the vast amount of information available on the Internet has made this much easier. Moreover, historical timetables are usually easily located for specific lines or locations, whilst for the more generalized models all you need do is to choose one or two places, the character of whose rail services you are seeking to model. For example, if you were modelling 'a typical Mosel valley station', the DB timetable for the Koblenz to Trier line for the relevant period would yield almost all the service information you require.

Freight trains are rather more problematic. There are many useful websites run by and for enthusiasts. For example, www.drehscheibe-online.de is an excellent portal, with many general information forums devoted to specific aspects, for example Alpine lines, goods train times and links to other sources of information.

Once again, membership of societies such as the Austrian Railway Group, German Railway Society, SNCF Society or Swiss Railway Society enables modellers to access fellow members' knowledge, which is usually considerable, especially through e-groups. The recently founded European Railways Association provides an additional dimension and source of shared information, particularly for those who are interested in the less-frequently modelled countries.

Finally, site research visits are for most of us far from difficult and budget airlines have greatly reduced their cost. It is often feasible to visit a chosen location for just a few pounds and time need not be an impediment, as day trips are by no means impossible if you live within striking distance of an airport. Eurostar is another option.

Once you have assembled the information, constructing a timetable is merely a matter of an evening or two's work. The main limiting factor for many will be ensuring that the layout has sufficient storage tracks. With your timetable compiled, then it is a simple case of doing a dry run to make sure that you have the space available for all your intended services. Often this will identify a need to make minor adjustments, or perhaps to reduce train lengths and so on. Not many of us can run eleven-coach or thirty-wagon trains in any scale!

Finally, you will need to decide whether to run to 'real time', to a speeded-up clock, or to adopt a sequence basis, with trains simply following each other in the correct order. And you need never get bored; once you have operated your full timetable a few times, simply introducing a late-running or extra 'special' can require some quick thinking if the remainder of your service is not to be disrupted. Again, just like the real thing!

CHAPTER SEVEN

MAKING THE EUROPEAN LANDSCAPE

There are many products available to reproduce the European landscape in miniature.

The landscape varies widely in Europe as a whole, from mountains to sun-drenched coastal areas. The enormity of the choices of areas to model is just one of the decisions open to the European railway modeller.

MAKING THE LANDFORMS

The foundation materials that are suitable for building a European layout depend upon:

- The scale of the landscape that you want to reproduce in miniature. The taller the scenery (such as Alpine rock faces), the stronger the support for the scenery will need to be

- Is the layout to be portable or permanent? If the layout is to be portable, it needs to be both strong but also light in weight, because if the landscape is to be covered in trees, buildings, rock faces and so on it is likely to become heavy. Scenery that is simply foliage or grass will be a lot lighter in weight. The more weight that will need to be supported, the stronger the land contours and the scenery foundations will need to be

- For portable layouts, if the scenery is likely to be heavy (such as modelled rock faces from plaster), consideration should be given to using detachable sections of scenery. Of course, the joins between the baseboard and the detachable scenery will need to be as good as possible.

A classic Swiss view of the Kandertal Valley in the Bernese Oberland taken in 2007 before most of the trains now using the Lötschberg route were diverted through the BLS AlpTransit tunnel.

ABOVE: *You could say that the blue of the river is too good to be true, but the camera does not lie. Here, a regional service from Interlaken to Spiez crosses the river that links Lakes Brienz and Thun in June 2007.*

RIGHT: *A double-track curved stone-built viaduct made solely from Heki materials.*

This aerial view of a double-track main line is another piece of good modelling by the folks at Heki.

MAKING THE CONTOURS OF THE LAND

The landscape needs good, firm support on any layout and once the size of the layout is determined, consideration needs to be given to the materials to be used in the construction of the baseboard and landscape. A good baseboard gives the trains the best possible chance of running well. Derailments can cause frustration and might ultimately lead someone to leave the hobby. There are many good books and DVDs available about how to make baseboards. We do not all need to have an A level in carpentry, because building baseboards is a skill that can be learnt.

Whilst layout builders will use their favourite timber for the baseboard and framework of the layout, there is an increasing choice of materials when it comes to the making the perimeter contours of the land to form the rear and side edges to any layout. Land contours can be made from:

- timber, including hardboard, plywood, oriented strand board, Sundeala or MDF available from DIY stores
- thick cardboard such as mounting card that is readily available from art shops or Hobbycraft
- polystyrene blocks that come as packing around white goods such as televisions, or household roof insulation foam material that is available from builder's merchants and DIY stores
- a selection of proprietary layout building materials such as the Busch Scenery Building system with honeycomb bases, or hard foam, the Noch Terra-Form system and the Woodland Scenics SubTerrain system.

Austria offers the potential to model narrow-gauge and standard-gauge trains from the same station. Here, an HO standard-gauge ÖBB Desiro Class 5022 2 car unit by Piko and a Pinzganau HOe narrow-gauge driving trailer by Liliput are used to see what potential such a layout might have.

LEFT: *Early stage of an Austrian layout. In the foreground the Woodland Scenics Track-Bed is seen, which deadens the noise of passing trains. The sharp edge will be covered with scenic materials.*

BELOW: *While some European countries feature flat countryside – the Benelux countries spring to mind – there are many areas of hilly and mountainous country involving train lines using viaducts, bridges and tunnels. This is one corner of a nicely crafted diorama by Heki.*

Featuring a railway line midway up the layout is a good way to make it visually interesting. Here, a Piko ÖBB Class 5022 unit stands above a retaining wall made from Heki flexible walling material.

The formers of the contours of the land need to be cut to the desired shape. Depending upon the type of material used for the landscape formers, they may either be cut with a saw, a jigsaw or a sharp craft knife. When using timber or card for the land contours, it is necessary to use intermediate supporting land contours at approximately 15cm intervals. The contour sections can be fixed to the baseboard with PVA woodworking adhesive, or by using a hot-glue gun for a quicker fix. Masking tape can be used to hold the upright land contours in place whilst the PVA glue dries – joints fixed with hot glue may need no support except from your hand for a few seconds.

RAISING THE TRACKBED ABOVE THE BASEBOARD

There are various methods of raising the track above a level baseboard, including dropping certain sections of the baseboard level in order to create a valley so that the higher trackbed can then run on a bridge, a viaduct or an embankment using a plywood base for the raised trackbed sitting on timber blocks. The Woodland Scenics SubTerrain range of hard foam pieces enables inclines and a raised trackbed to be made quickly using lightweight materials. Another alternative is open baseboard construction, which can accommodate changes in the land formation by the use of shaped contour formers.

Felled trees on the slope behind the passing train give the impression of a recently cleared area. The bases of the felled trees were made from small twigs that were cut down and then pushed into holes in the plaster cloth that formed the basis of the landscape.

RIGHT: Noch's range of laser-cut bridge kits made from cardboard is useful in a number of scales. When I first learned that they were made from cardboard I was dubious about their strength. My fears were ungrounded, because once assembled they are strong and they do look good too.

BELOW LEFT: Raising the track above a flat baseboard is one way to improve the appearance of a layout. At the Bergun Museum in Graubünden, Switzerland, there are very well made landscape foundations for an O-scale layout.

ABOVE: The narrow-gauge Rhätische Bahn darts in and out of tunnels, which will be represented here in Om form at the Bergun Museum.

ABOVE LEFT: This layout has arguably some of the best-quality foundations I have ever seen, using good-quality timber that will not fall down in a hurry.

ABOVE RIGHT: One section of the Bergun Museum layout showing the subtle colours used on the scenic side of the layout.

FILLING THE SPACE BETWEEN THE LAND CONTOURS

Once the contour formers have been shaped and fixed to the baseboards, thought needs to be given as to how to fill in the space between the land contours. A large number of methods include the Busch dedicated landscape system that incorporates heavy-duty crêpe paper, which can be fixed to the landscape formers with a staple gun or hot glue.

Chicken wire is one of the traditional methods, being spread between, and then fixed to, the top of the timber contour formers. A light steel mesh that can be bought from a car repair shop or sold as a model railway product by Busch, Noch or other firms is an alternative to chicken wire.

Noch's Terra-Form System uses timber dowel posts and fixing plugs to produce a lightweight basis for the hills, embankments and tunnels.

Polystyrene blocks or foam pieces (similar to that used in home roof insulation) can be carved with a sharp knife to fill the landscape. The Woodland Scenics SubTerrain system, with its multiple pieces of polystyrene hard foam sheets and sectional pieces, offers a comprehensive landscaping system that includes dedicated adhesives, tools, instruction books and DVDs.

A web of strips of corrugated card or masking tape can be fixed to timber formers and to each other using hot glue or a staple gun. The closer together the tape, the stronger the web will be to take plaster-impregnated cloth or similar. Crumpled newspaper or parcel packing can also be pushed between the contour formers and then covered with plaster-impregnated cloth.

Plaster-impregnated cloth is deservedly popular with scenery builders. It is available at many model shops under various names, including Mod-Roc, Peco Landform and Woodland Scenics Plaster Cloth and is sold by others, including DoubleO Scenics, Gaugemaster, Geoscenics, Heki, Noch and so on. It needs to be cut into manageable pieces and after wetting it can be laid over crumpled newspaper or any of the other suggested materials above and smoothed down with the fingers. One or two layers are sufficient to give a good basis for the landscape. The Plaster Cloth Modelling Tray by Woodland Scenics is ideal for wetting cut pieces of plaster cloth, but you could arguably do that in a bucket. What is good about this piece of equipment is that it is non-stick and after you have finished working with plaster cloth just rinse the tray out with warm soapy water and it is as good as new.

A plastic kit by Kibri was used to make this bridge over a gorge. Plaster cloth was used to shape the landscape and Noch lightweight hard foam pieces were used for the supporting piers.

Once the plaster cloth was painted green and covered with Woodland Scenics Poly Fibre, the rocky outcrops by Noch were added. A footpath was made a little higher than the stream in the valley.

A BLS Re 4/4 Class 420 by Roco crosses the girder bridge pulling a carriage by Liliput.

In a different location the same plastic girder bridge by Kibri was used to cross a deep valley with a waterfall flowing nearby. The loco is an ÖBB Hercules Class 2016 by Piko.

MODELLING A LASER-CUT BRIDGE

A Piko SNCF Fret-liveried Vossloh locomotive 461006 crosses the river bridge with a mixed freight service. The staining on the side of the bridge panels was a few drops of weathering dye brushed into the corner of the panels. The rust effect spread as the dye soaked into the cardboard.

The components of Noch bridge 67050. The bridge is HO scale, with all the parts of the bridge made from laser-cut card except for the two supporting pillars, which are pre-coloured hard foam pieces. The kit comes complete with a tube of the recommended UHU Holz Leim quick-drying adhesive for assembly. The instructions are mainly pictorial.

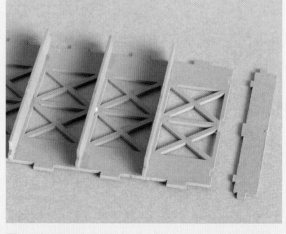

The side pieces of the bridge feature several 'nicks' of cardboard that need to be cut through to release the sections of cardboard from the backing sheet. Here is the underside of the bridge once some of the supporting cross-members have been added. I found that the various pieces of the kit went very well together. They all fitted snugly and only needed a small amount of adhesive to fix them together. The last supporting cross-member is still to be added in this picture.

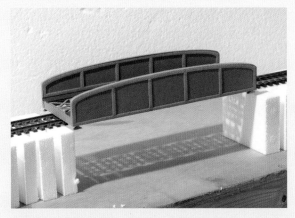

ABOVE LEFT: The bridge in place on the (under construction) layout before the pillars were installed. The bridge is seen in its clean, unweathered state.

ABOVE RIGHT: The hard foam pillars are easy to cut down to the height of the trackbed with a sharp craft knife and steel ruler. The bridge kit comes complete with these bridge pillars.

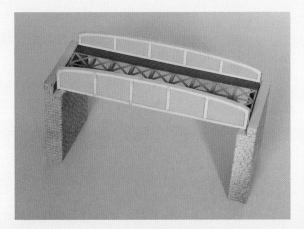

ABOVE LEFT: A nearly completed bridge fits snugly on the supporting bridge pillars made from hard foam.

ABOVE RIGHT: The bridge pillars were blended into the landscape using a mixture of rocks and foliage. On both sides of the bridge there are rocks – these were made from Noch hard foam pieces, which simply had to be cut with a sharp craft knife and made to fit the location. Any gaps were filled in using Heki foliage material.

CHAPTER EIGHT

ROCKS

Rock faces, cliffs and mountainsides are common in Europe.

Many European layouts require rock faces, rocks on the landscape or cliffs. These might include a mountainous line, or a line hugging the coastline such as between Marseille and Nice. There is a huge variety of products available to reproduce rocks in miniature.

There are various well-established methods of making rocks and rock faces, including cork bark that is readily available from garden centres and model shops. Some modellers still use this material and if it is sufficiently 'bedded in' with foliage or talus (small rocks), it looks quite effective. If its natural colour does not reflect the location of your layout it can be painted by building up layers of thin washes of acrylic paints. Products such as Polyfilla or other household plaster mixes are readily available from DIY stores and when sculpted with an old knife and then painted with acrylics these can look good too.

There are numerous rock compounds available from all the main scenery manufacturers such as those illustrated here.

In addition, there is also an increasing number of proprietary model railway scenery products on the market to make rocks and rock faces from companies including Busch, Faller, Heki, Noch, Woodlands Scenics and others. Most of these products are easy to use and with a little practice the results are good. Both Noch and Woodland Scenics make starter kits for making rocks. These provide a good way to learn how to use these techniques.

LOOKING AT THE REAL THING

Before considering how to make a rocky outcrop on your layout, it is best to study photographs of prototype rock faces for the area that you are modelling, because rock strata and colours are very different throughout Europe. Some rocks are light in colour, whilst other rocks such as granite are darker in colour. All rock types have distinctive rock formations; some are smooth, whilst others are very brittle and fragmented.

USING BUSCH ROCK-SCULPTING COMPOUND

Various companies make rock-sculpting compound, including Busch, Faller, Green Scene, Noch and Woodland Scenics. The technique is explained below using a Busch product, but a similar step-by-step procedure will apply to all the products. These modelling compounds are useful when working with other products such as the cork bark, Heki Rock Foil and Noch Hard Foam pieces to blend the rock pieces into the landscape.

The powder compound needs to be mixed with a little water until it forms a creamy compound. Follow the instructions on the packet to get the mix right.

*RIGHT: **This finished rock face has good subdued colouring, plus well-made fissures. I fully recommend a visit to the Bergun Museum to see this splendid layout. The museum is located directly at Bergun station on the RhB line between Chur and St Moritz.***

*BOTTOM LEFT: **Busch modelling compound was mixed with the prescribed amount of water with a wooden stick.***

*BOTTOM MIDDLE: **A little PVA adhesive was added to the modelling compound to help it to stick better to the underlying landscape.***

*BOTTOM RIGHT: **The sculpting compound was spread on top of the dried plaster cloth with a wooden lollipop stick. This stick can also be used to shape the rock faces.***

If you add too much water the mixture will be too sloppy and will not set. I also mix in a little PVA glue because I find that this will help it fix to the landscape more firmly and quickly. Then spread the mixed compound on to the area to be treated with an old kitchen knife or a flat wooden stick. Push it into the landscape so that it has a firm fix and as the mixture begins to dry sculpt the rock face with an old knife or a wooden lollipop stick. The material begins to set within fifteen minutes, but stays workable for about two hours, drying fully in a couple of days (this time is dependent upon the general weather and the temperature in the room in which the layout is located).

Once the mixture is dry, the surface can be painted using diluted acrylic paints, Woodland Scenics Earth Colour Liquid Pigments or weathering dyes, using several thin washes rather than one thick coat. Use dry-brushing techniques to highlight the strata effect in the rocks and leave to dry. The horizontal sections of the rock faces can be treated with scatter materials and/or static grass to represent grass and weeds growing in the crevices and fissures.

The finished rock face after all the shaping had been done. It was then left to dry fully overnight – drying will take longer if the layout is in a cold, damp environment.

Once the modelling compound had fully dried, a light grey first coat of paint was spray-painted on, using a Humbrol acrylic aerosol.

Small stones and rocks were added from a bag of garden footpath gravel. I chose the smallest pieces, fixing them down by dribbling diluted PVA over them and waiting for them to dry.

Green acrylic spray paint from an aerosol was added in some places to create the base colour for the grass and weeds.

RIGHT: Static grass fibres were planted over the green paint and the tunnel mouth and retaining walls by Noch were fitted into the landscape.

BELOW: A BLS Robel track-maintenance vehicle by Kibri stands amidst mountain scenery made using hard foam pieces as the landscape foundations.

USING DRY PLASTER

Most of us have some Polyfilla or similar DIY plaster products in our garage or shed and these can be used successfully to make rock faces. Always mix the plaster in accordance with the manufacturer's instructions and if you want a quicker result choose a ready-mixed product that can be used straight from the tube.

It is advisable to use several thin layers of the mixed plaster material to build up a rock face rather than just one layer, because in my experience one thick layer will not dry so well as several thinner layers. Mix a little PVA adhesive with the plaster with the prescribed quantity of water, as this will help the mixture to stick to the underlying landscape. I then 'paint' PVA on to the landscape foundation before coating it with mixed plaster to ensure that the mixed plaster firmly fixes to the landscape. When the plaster is mixed into a smooth but sticky substance, an old kitchen knife, an obsolete modelling knife, or a flat wooden stick can be used to 'push' the mixed plaster on to the landscape. Allow each layer to dry fully before adding the next layer.

A minute or so after putting on the final coating of plaster on to the landscape, shape it whilst it is still damp. Use pictures of real rocks and sculpt the rock into the formation in your pictures. Are the real rocks fissured, broken or crumbling? Try to reproduce the appropriate effect and once the plaster is fully dry (usually the next day, but will be longer if the weather is damp), use a variety of acrylic paints, weathering dyes or Woodland Scenics Earth Colour Liquid Pigments to 'paint' the rocks. Run thin washes of colour over them and once the initial paint has dried, dry-brush darker and lighter shades to give the rocks contrast and depth.

USING HEKI ROCK FOIL

Heki produces rock foil sections that are coloured plastic-based sheets that have a ripple effect and come ready painted and highlighted to represent various types of rock. These rock foil sheets are sold in pieces 18 × 40cm and 35 × 80cm in slate, dolomite, stone, sandstone and granite colours, as well as different strata shapes. The material is very strong but pliable and can be moulded between your fingers.

The sheets are easy to use by cutting the piece with craft scissors to cover the area that you need on the landscape. The piece can then be fixed to the landscape using a hot-glue gun, a staple gun or PVA glue. Use a rock-sculpting mix or DIY plaster filler to blend the edge of the piece into the rest of the landscape. Use acrylic paints to enhance the rock foil further, then use dry-brushing techniques to highlight the rugged nature of the strata. This is a lightweight method of adding rock faces to a layout.

USING NOCH HARD FOAM

Noch produces pieces of rock to represent granite, sandstone and slate. These three types of rock pieces are made from hard foam that is light in weight, easy to use and ready coloured. The rock pieces need to be cut off the backing board with a sharp craft knife, which is very easy to do. It is advisable to cut the rocks over a cutting board. There are four or five rock pieces in each pack, but the rocks can be reduced in size to make more rocks by dividing (cutting) the rock pieces using a fret saw or a long, sharp blade.

The rock sections can then be glued to the scenery using PVA or hot glue. Leave overnight to allow the glue to dry fully. The rock pieces can be moulded into the landscape by using modelling compound (Busch, Faller, Noch or Woodland Scenics Hydrocal) around the edges of the rock pieces and again leave this to dry overnight. Once the rocks are fully set, they can be weathered with acrylic paints and stains, or alternatively they can be left in their natural colour.

USING WOODLAND SCENICS ROCK MOULDS

Rock pieces of varying sizes can be made using Woodland Scenics Lightweight Hydrocal and Rock Moulds; the latter are flexible rubber pieces that are shaped into different rock shapes and sizes. This technique works the same way as making jelly by pouring the mix into the mould, leaving it to dry for a while, then taking out a hardened piece that mirrors the mould. Choose those that are the most suitable rock

SNCF X73500 by Jouef in HO scale out in the countryside. The bridge is a laser-cut kit by Noch and the pieces of rock are hard foam sections that come ready coloured and shaped, also by Noch.

moulds for your layout. See the choice available in the Woodland Scenics catalogue, or its website at www. woodlandscenics.com.

Mix the Hydrocal as directed on the instructions in a mixing bowl that is used only for scenic work. Stir it well until all the powder is mixed thoroughly with the water and be careful to follow precisely the suggested quantities in the instructions. Wet the inside of the rubber mould with water and a few drops of washing-up liquid, as this will stop the Hydrocal mixture sticking to the mould as it dries.

Pour the mix into the mould, ensuring that it fully covers the indented shape of the mould, but do not overfill the top edge of the mould. Tap the sides of the rubber mould lightly to dislodge any bubbles of air that are in the mix. Leave the mould somewhere warm to dry and after about one hour (on a very damp day this might take longer; on a very hot day this might take less time) 'peel' away the mould from the rocks, then leave the rock piece to harden fully overnight before moving on to the next stage.

Do not be surprised if some of the rock pieces break as they come out of the mould. It does happen, however carefully you try to release the rocks. This will not matter too much, because you may be able to get two rocks for the price of one and they can be used together or independently.

Once the rock sections are fully dry, fix the rock pieces to the landscape using PVA or hot glue, then leave them to set overnight. To blend the rocks into the landscape, mix up some more Hydrocal and 'brush' it around the rock pieces so that the rocks do not look as if they have been just 'plonked' on to the landscape. Once all the rocks are dry, paint thin washes of acrylic paints or Woodland Scenics Earth Colour Liquid Pigments over the rock face in different colours to highlight the crevices and so on. Hide the edges of the rocks with scatter materials, foliage, polyfibre or Woodland Scenics Fine Leaf Foliage.

FINISHING TIPS FOR ROCK FACES

In real life, pieces of a rock face break off and fall to the bottom. Model this in miniature by using small broken pieces of the main rocks, colouring them the same as the main rocks, then 'plant' a few weeds in them. At the bottom of a rock face or cliff it is worth sprinkling a few small natural stones (this is usually known as talus and is available from Faller, Noch, Woodland Scenics and others) to represent debris and fallen rocks. Alternatively, see what is available in your garden and fix these pieces to the scene using PVA adhesive.

Where rock faces and grass banks join, undergrowth and weeds will add to the visual appearance. Taller grasses (available from Woodlands Scenics, Noch, miniNatur and others) placed near the base of a rock face and finished with dabs of scatter material will give the scenery a little more texture. Rubberized horsehair or old brush bristles may be useful as tall grasses and brambles.

Making rock faces needs to be done over several days – the rock material, the adhesive and the paint all need drying time. A hot-glue gun speeds up the scenery-making process. Another method is to use some of the rock compound to fix the rocks to the landscape.

Weather the rock pieces in several stages by using thin washes of different shades of colour, so that a 3-D effect results. Allow a little darker wash to trickle through the crevices. Use similar colours and types of rocks on a layout. It is very rare to see different types of rock within a small area.

A Traxx locomotive in Zebra livery by Piko enters the tunnel on the author's diorama.

An autumn scene on an Austrian single-track line. The leaves on the trackside foliage are changing, as are the leaves on the trees but not those on the evergreen conifers. The weeds are tinged with brown as the summer has reached its end.

The station of Cavaglia as modelled by Stephan Kraus is truly set in autumn because of the colours of the needles on the larch trees. This project, built to celebrate the Bernina centenary, took Stephan four months to build, spending 598 hours in total. There are over 250 trees on the layout, which were all handmade and requiring about ten minutes per tree to build. The autumn colouring on the entire layout is very well done, because the colour tones are natural.

continued overleaf

ABOVE LEFT: *Bushes, weeds, grass and trees all change colour in the autumn. Subtle colours are needed so that the effect is not too gaudy. Here, Stephan Kraus has captured the colours well.*

ABOVE RIGHT: *More larch trees to convey the appearance of the month of October in the Alps.*

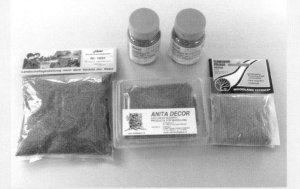

ABOVE: *Various companies retail subdued scatter material for the landscape and leaves. Treemendus is one such company. At the top of the picture is a piece of its 'teddy-bear fur', which could be used to represent tired tall grasses on the lineside.*

ABOVE RIGHT: *When I started to look around for autumn-coloured scatter and leaf material, I soon realized that more is available than I had anticipated. Here is a selection by Anita Décor, Heki, Polak and Woodland Scenics.*

RIGHT: *Some ready to plant models of trees with autumn foliage do not look particularly realistic. This one by Woodland Scenics may look all right in the forest of Maine in 'The Fall', but the foliage is too thick and too intense to my eye.*

 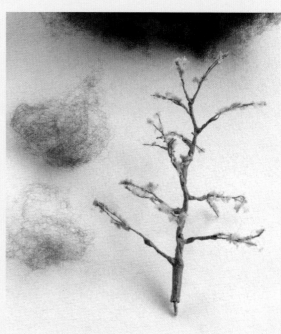

ABOVE LEFT: **I pulled off the foliage between my fingers, which took less than five minutes.**

ABOVE RIGHT: **Some of the bits of the original foliage were left on the branches, but this did not matter because they would be covered with new foliage. I teased out some brown polyfibre material (www.micromark.com) that I had to hand to represent the new foliage.**

After the new foliage was teased out and glued on to the branches, I lightly sprayed the tree with extra-hold unscented hairspray. Then I sprinkled on autumn leaves and here is the result.

continued overleaf

ABOVE LEFT: *These overhanging bushes have started to lose their leaves, which have fallen on the platform.*

ABOVE RIGHT: *Mehano SNCB 7738 locomotive was filmed by rail enthusiasts on 21 October 2014 somewhere in Belgium. The weeds along the track were originally summer green, but I dragged a paintbrush with light brown acrylic paint on them across the tops of the grasses.*

The changing colour of the leaves on the trees, the grass and fallen leaves establishes this as an autumn scene.

CHAPTER NINE

TREES FOR EUROPEAN LAYOUTS

Europe has a lot of trees and plenty are needed on layouts too!

Over 36 per cent of the land surface of the European Community is covered in trees that fall into two types: conifers and broad-leaved. With over one-third of the land area of the Southern Alps almost half-covered with forests, there can never be too many trees on a European layout. Trees can be modelled in a variety of different ways, including single-specimen trees (maybe near the front of the layout) that need to be modelled in full and trees in a woodland or forest that sometimes only need to be modelled on one side or the top where the trees are closely planted within a clump of trees.

READY-TO-PLANT TREES

There are a good number of model tree manufacturers that make model trees that are good representations of real trees, whilst others are not. A piece of lichen stuck on to a shiny plastic trunk or a bottle-brush tree that does not look like a conifer are not going to add to the realism of a layout. Generally, the more one pays for model trees, usually the better the model will be. The main manufacturers of mass-produced models of European trees are 4D Model Shop, Busch, Faller, Gaugemaster, Heki, Noch, The Model Tree Shop and Woodland Scenics. Many of these tree ranges include packs of snow-covered trees for winter scenes. The Model Tree Shop retails various tree ranges, including string and wire, plastic trunks, etched brass and twisted wire, with a product range from entry-level trees to beautifully made trees for Z through to O scale.

Manufacturers usually retail basic and 'premium' ranges, with the premium trees sold singly or in packs of two, three or five, depending upon the type of tree and the size. Many firms, including Busch,

The quality of ready-to-plant trees from the big manufacturers such as Busch, Heki and Noch is improving with each new introduction. Here is a selection of the latest fir trees from Noch. Their foliage is 'light and fluffy', which looks more realistic compared with cheaper bottle-brush trees.
NOCH

Gaugemaster, Heki and Noch, retail bumper bags of coniferous trees that usually represent good value. By trimming any ragged pieces off the branches on bottle-brush coniferous trees, then lightly painting on PVA adhesive and sprinkling on good-quality fine scatter material the appearance can be greatly improved.

Woodland Scenics has a vast range of tree products. These include ready-made trees and tree kits. Their Fine-Leaf Foliage is ideal for smaller trees and their tree armatures (these form the trunk and branches) are available in various sizes in metal and plastic. The various foliage products are sold in a range of colours from spring green through to autumn tints.

There are several European manufacturers that retail exquisite trees, though these do come at a cost compared to bulk tree packs. These are available

Heki's fir trees now have foliage that uses delicate fibres, which can be used either as foreground or distant trees.

If you are modelling a line in the south of France, you will need olive trees. These are now available from Heki, Noch and other companies. This scene by Noch includes its lavender strips to complete the scene.
NOCH

from Anita Décor, Langmesser Modellwelt, miniNatur and Model Scene.

Companies that specialize in architectural models manufacture good-quality trees and where the budget permits these would be ideal for single standing specimen trees and those near to the viewing edge of a layout. These companies include 4D Model Shop and Treemendus Models.

BIRCH

Most tree manufacturers make representations of birch trees, but some of the best are by Anita Décor. Their handmade silver birch trees are sold in various heights and feature a treated trunk that is a natural plant material with added foliage. The texture and colour of the bark is superb and the foliage is airy. If your budget does not run to a number of these trees, then buy just one or two specimen trees for the foreground on your layout.

DEAD TREES

Hedgerow Scenics produces models of dead trees for N and HO scales. Real twigs form the trunk and branches of the tree, then are covered with fine foliage on the lower section to represent ivy and other creeping vegetation, with a planting pin for fixing the tree to the landscape. The colour of the foliage and leaf effect is realistic and subdued. These would look good positioned on the edge of a field or railway line and because the trees use natural material they look very realistic.

FALLING TREES

Noch makes a falling tree for HO scale to add a lot of realism to a forestry scene. It can be operated either manually by an on/off switch, or by digital control. The decoder is programmed to let the tree fall realistically, so that initially it falls slowly, then gets then faster and faster as it heads towards the ground. When it reaches the ground, it bounces slightly and after a few seconds returns to the upright position. The Digital Tree has a decoder that automatically recognizes the Märklin®/Motorola and DCC/NMRA formats and can use a locomotive address using a 16V AC/DC power supply.

FIR TREES

Commonly seen throughout most of Europe, there are various varieties of fir tree and in model form the quality of them is improving all the time. Anita Décor, Heki, miniNatur and Noch firs are all of very good quality, with light foliage and subtle colours. To go that extra mile in realism, Busch produces packs of fir trees that feature add-on fir cones. The cones are just a couple of millimetres long and can be attached to the underside of the branches using all-purpose adhesive. These packs generally contain two fir trees and are sold in different heights.

LARCH TREES

Larch trees (*Larix* species) are one of the most common conifer trees to be seen in Europe. Whilst they are conifers, they are also deciduous and are one of the earliest trees to green up in spring and in autumn give a good display of colour. The distinctive feature of larches is that their long lower branches spread with a downward bounce, with the tips turning up. Larches grow up to 40m or more in height and the trees have cones up to about 10cm long.

Heki makes both ready-assembled trees and kits of larch trees in HO scale. The trees and trunk pieces come as a mid-brown plastic, which is best painted to remove the sheen of the plastic. The texture of the foliage material is rather unusual – it feels like chopped-up pieces of a nylon pan-scrubbing pad. To fix the foliage material to the trunk and branches, use PVA glue brushed on to both sides of the tree and with the glue on the tree dip the tree into the foliage material, turn it over and then sprinkle on foliage material to any branches that had not caught the foliage material. Most other companies make models of larch trees too, of which some of the best quality are by miniNatur.

SCOTS PINES

4D Model Shop, miniNatur and The Model Tree Shop retail good models of Scots pine trees in a number of different heights and these will add some variety to the predominance of conifers. The trees are usually made from twisted fine wire, with fine web foliage mat representing the leaves. The bark is covered with material to bulk it up and to disguise the twisted wires.

Before you begin to make any models of trees, it is always good to look at a few reference books to gain a little more background information.

BUILDING A GOOD-QUALITY TREE KIT

As we have mentioned, there is a large variety of decent quality ready-to-plant trees available from model shops today, but if you want very good-quality specimen trees on your layout should you buy them or make them? Some cottage industry tree manufacturers such as Ceynix and Treemendus make trees to specific requirements. 4D Model Shop offers very high-quality tree models too.

One company that makes an excellent quality range of trees is German manufacturer miniNatur, producing tree kits of various types in a number of heights and seasonal foliage colours. The range includes Alpine conifers and firs, Mediterranean trees and the more familiar beech and oaks. Their models are not cheap, but in my experience they are certainly some of the best-quality trees that can be bought in ready-made or kit form. The tree kits come with mainly pictorial instructions and the accompanying step by step sequence of pictures and captions covers all the stages of the building process of a weathered larch for HO scale. The kits are fun to make and the end result is realistic. It takes

about two hours to build one tree, but if you were setting up a production line to build these trees it would take less time, because as the glue sets on the branches of one tree you could be working on the next tree and so on.

It is definitely worth spending a few minutes looking through the supplied diagrams before starting to make a tree kit so that you can avoid any pitfalls. Trees like this are best suited to be specimen trees in the foreground of layouts.

The following pictures show how to build a miniNatur tree kit. The trunk and branches in the miniNatur kit come as one flat armature, which is light in weight and easy to bend. The tree illustrated here is 16.5cm tall and is intended for HO scale. The entire tree armature is covered in bark effect and painted in various shades of brown and grey. The base of the tree has a screw thread for fixing to a layout.

ABOVE: Close-up of the bark texture on the miniNatur tree armature, which is very realistic.

RIGHT: The first step is to hold the base of the tree armature in one hand and bend the branches in different directions, which is a five-minute job. It is very easy to bend the branches into various directions; just make sure that the branches go in all directions so that the tree has a full 3-D effect.

The tree armature will look like this when you have twisted all of the branches into the correct shape.

Each weathered spruce tree kit comes with a tree armature and two pieces of foliage – one green and the other brown. I found that I needed only about 75 per cent of both foliage mats when making the tree and I have kept the rest of the material for other projects. Small scissors were used to cut the foliage mat into pieces and tweezers were used to push the foliage mat into the glue on the branches. UHU Holz Leim was one of the adhesives used because it is quick-drying.

LEFT: When the foliage mats are teased out they look like this, with a pen shown to give some idea of scale. Cut across the mat so that the strands of material will hang down on the branches. By the way, the scissors need to be sharp – one pair of scissors that I had to hand was no good at cutting the mat at all!

ABOVE LEFT: *Here is the spread adhesive just before a piece of the foliage was pushed into the adhesive. I used Deluxe Materials R/C Modellers Craft Glue and UHU Holz Leim to fix the foliage on to the branches, because I found that both adhesives set quickly and dry clear matt. I used a small wooden coffee stirrer to spread the glue on to one side of a branch.*

ABOVE RIGHT: *A piece of foliage mat has been pushed into the wet glue on one of the upper branches. The length of the trailing foliage will be cut down once the glue has dried.*

ABOVE LEFT: *I treated about six to eight branches at a time. The foliage will be trimmed with scissors once the adhesive has dried. The branches need to be adjusted between the fingers to portray the drooping arch of branches of a spruce tree.*

ABOVE RIGHT: *On some of the lower branches, I used brown foliage to represent dead branches and foliage. The longer lengths would be cut off once the glue has set.*

The completed weathered spruce tree with a mixture of brown and green foliage, which is the result of two hours' work.

(www.mininatur.de). The website has both English and German text. Their product catalogues, price lists and instruction leaflets are all available on the website and in the UK the trees can be purchased from International Models and other retailers.

Tree kits are made by a number of other companies, including Green Scene, Heki, Noch, Treemendus and Woodland Scenics.

This sequence of four pictures demonstrates how to make Heki larch tree kits. The Heki tree kit comes with ten plastic tree armatures, plus a bag of foliage texture material. I kept the plastic 'bubble' to keep the foliage material in as I applied it to the branches. Deluxe Materials Scatter Grip is one of the adhesives that can be used to fix the foliage material on to the tree armature. I used the Fine Turf to fill in any tiny gaps not covered with foliage material.

The following tools and materials will be needed:

- small pair of sharp scissors to cut the foliage mat
- wooden coffee stirrer to apply the glue on to the branches to take the foliage
- Deluxe Materials R/C Modellers Craft Glue or UHU Holz Leim or PVA adhesive
- fine good-quality dark brown scatter material
- pair of tweezers to position the foliage on to the adhesive.

If you would like to know more about miniNatur products, the entire range can be seen on its website

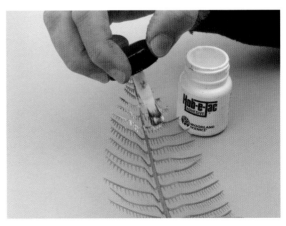

To fix the foliage material to the trunk I used Hob-e-Tac glue brushed on to both sides of the trunk.

ABOVE LEFT: With the glue on the trunk, I dipped the trunk into the foliage material, turned the trunk over, then sprinkled on foliage material to any branches that had not caught foliage material.

ABOVE RIGHT: Five completed larch trees from the Heki kit left to dry by standing their trunks in a block of polystyrene.

TOP TIPS FOR MAKING A MININATUR TREE KIT

- Do not use contact adhesive to fix the foliage on to the branches, because it leaves a shine on the branches.
- Fingers can very sticky with glue, so it is necessary to wash them frequently during the assembly process.
- Remember to cut the foliage mat so that the trailing foliage hangs down on the tree.
- I found that both Deluxe Materials R/C Modellers Craft Glue and UHU Holz Leim set quickly and dried clear matt. PVA adhesive takes longer to dry.
- There is no need to cover every branch with foliage. Branches without foliage look like dead branches.
- MiniNatur sells the excellent foliage material separately if you choose to use tree armatures by different companies.
- Making an armature yourself with wire or balsa wood is not that difficult, so that you could make your own larch trees using the miniNatur foliage mat.

MAKING THE FOREST FLOOR

When planting trees on a layout, it is worth considering the landscape into which the trees will be planted. In a dense forest very little vegetation grows beneath the trees, but if the trees are planted singly or widely spaced, then shrubs, flowers, weeds, tall grasses and dead branches will litter the soil beneath the trees. There are various products from Heki, miniNatur, Noch, Scenic Express, Train Terrain, Treemendus, Woodland Scenics and WW Scenics that can be used to make the forest floor or the area beneath trees look very realistic.

Below trees, the ground is generally not green unless the trees are sparsely planted. So a fine foam material such as Woodland Scenics brown Fine Turf sprinkled on top of spread PVA glue would look good, with the odd weed or two represented by grass tufts. The tufts can be removed from their packaging with tweezers and then a spot of adhesive dabbed on the base to fix them to the landscape; either PVA or hot glue is ideal for this purpose.

Packs of grass tufts are sold in spring, summer, autumn and flowering colours to suit the season modelled on your layout.

Another alternative to represent the forest floor is the miniNatur range of grass mats, including forest floor mats that are sold in two colours (summer and autumn). The mats are suitable for OO scale upwards, with a predominantly brown foam mat containing random clumps of grass. Busch, Faller, Hedgerow Scenics, Langmesser Modellwelt, Model Scene and Noch also produce grass mats with grass fibres of various heights and textures. Some of the mats include bits of rock and twig, which are ideal to represent forest floors.

Treemendus Models and WW Scenics produce bags of real wood forest floor debris material that is easy to sprinkle over brushed-on PVA glue. For the underbrush near the edge of a forest, US scenic manufacturer Scenic Express makes a large range of Flock and Turf textures that include small pieces of twig in their mixes to represent a forest floor. To see more about the available colour and texture variations, go to www.scenicexpress. com and to obtain Scenic Express products in the UK go to www.modeljunction.info and other retailers.

Forest floor material is available from a number of manufacturers, including Busch, Scenic Express, Treemendus, Woodland Scenics and WW Scenics.

Garden twigs are useful to represent cut-down trees on a layout. The ends need to be cut carefully with a sharp small saw to look as realistic as possible. This scene was modelled by Stephan Kraus.

The tree stumps of felled trees look good on most layouts where there are trees. Cut twigs can be pushed into holes in the landscape and fixed with a small blob of PVA glue.

Busch produces a huge selection of scenic scatter materials in a variety of textures and colours to represent every season and that are suitable for all the popular scales. The choices include special sands, flock materials, scatters, micro-flocks, multi-coloured flocks, grass fibres and mixed packs in an enormous array of colours. Its four mixed-ground cover packs are designed for beach and park paths, forest tracks, deciduous forest floor and coniferous forest floor. The deciduous forest floor pack is made up of sand, gravel and green flock to represent the fairly open ground cover you would see below deciduous trees, especially in autumn and winter months. The material gives the effect of soil and dry fallen leaves. These packs are good value because rather than needing to buy three or four packs of different-coloured scatters to get the same effect, you only need to buy one pack of ready-mixed material.

To represent climbers on trees, miniNatur Ivy matting is available. It is a fine mesh with ivy-shaped leaves attached to it. The material is easy to tear off from the main piece to suit the area you need to

*Static grass fibres are a good way to elevate the look of a layout. These are now readily available for scales between N and O. There are a number of electrostatic tools to plant the fibres. For more information, see my book, **Railway Modelling Skills**, also published by Crowood.*

cover. It can be attached to tree trunks and walls with PVA or a similar adhesive.

Busch makes plastic ferns and mushrooms for OO/HO scale. Model Scene and Noch produce laser-cut card plants including ferns.

MODELLING TREES IN THE ALPS

Many modellers reproducing European railway scenes are drawn to the Alps because the scenery is glorious – mountains, lakes, trees, river gorges, rushing streams and wild flowers. Alpine architecture is attractive, including timber-built chalets, and who cannot help but be enthused by the sight of a locomotive and a chain of carriages making their way along a winding Alpine line.

The Alps are the largest mountain range in Europe, running from southern France in a wide arc for nearly 1,000km across Austria, northern Italy, southern Germany, Liechtenstein, Slovenia and Switzerland. The width of the Alpine arc is around 200km, with many mountains over 3,500m. The range peaks at Mont Blanc, at 4,807m above sea level.

The Alps have long formed an obstacle to European north–south travel, but mountain-climbing railways, tunnels (new and old), cable cars and funiculars have all contributed to the accessibility of the Alps for tourists today.

Modellers reproducing a part of the Alpine landscape will need a lot of trees, as deciduous trees, including beech and oak, can grow at altitudes of up to 1,300m. Coniferous trees, including pine, Scots pine and spruce, can grow at up to 1,900m above sea level.

In Austria, the percentage of production forests out of the total forested areas in mountainous areas is 57 per cent, which gives rise to accessibility difficulties, because many of these trees are located on steep terrain, with gradients of more than 30 per cent. Helicopters are often seen carrying tree trunks

Nr. 1673 Blätterbäume und Büsche
15 Stück herbstlich
autumnal leafy trees and bushes
arbres et buissons d'automne

Based on sea moss, Heki has a range of autumn trees with leaves that are changing colours. Tree manufacturers produce trees for all the seasons.

A Bemo HOm RhB Ge 4/4 III locomotive emerges through the edge of a forest.

away from difficult locations. In Switzerland, the tree population is split as follows: conifers (twelve species) 61 per cent; and broad-leaved trees (over forty species) 39 per cent. The Swiss forestry industry employs 90,000 people, with 30 per cent of the country covered in trees.

To give some idea of relative heights: a silver birch can grow up to 30m tall; Norway spruce up to 65m tall; Scots pines up to 35m; larch up to 35m; and silver fir up to 50m. By comparison, a Swiss SBB Class 460 Re 4/4 locomotive measures 4.31m from rail height to the top of its body and is 18.5m in length over its buffers.

TOP TIPS FOR MODELLING TREES

- Use different scenic materials on your trees and the ground cover. If scatter materials of similar colours are used on the trees and the landscape, the layout will look too uniform in colour. For example, lighter ground cover colours will contrast well with darker green trees.
- Plastic trunks can be too shiny, so need to be painted with matt acrylic paint or similar paints.
- Rather than limiting your trees to the uniform firs (that is, the bottle-brush variety), use other trees to add visual variety such as larches, which in spring have lighter green foliage compared to that of the fir and pine trees. Scots pine trees can be mixed with other varieties of coniferous tree for greater variety.
- Where the trees are 'planted' at the rear of the layout, use clumps of trees rather than single trees on the skyline to provide the impression of close-growing trees rather than random planting.
- Trees need to be of varying heights to reflect different ages and locations. In real life, some single standing trees near stations and chalets are very tall.
- Storms, heavy waters and avalanches can create hillsides and river valleys of devastation. Fallen trees and foliage litter these areas and these scenes can be created by using small twigs to represent tree stumps, fallen trees and dead wood.
- Because layouts need a lot of trees, buy the big bags of conifers for background trees. Improve their appearance by brushing on PVA adhesive, then sprinkling on fine-quality scatter materials.
- Use best-quality trees in the foreground to create the impression that all the trees on the layout are superb models!
- Trees are taller than we might think; for example, a silver birch tree can grow up to 30m tall and a Norway spruce can grow up to 65m.

To build up the edge of a forest, trees need to be quite tightly packed. Here, the types of tree have been mixed, but it still does not give the illusion of a deep forest. To the left on the ground various dark scatter material has been sprinkled on PVA adhesive as a 'forest floor cover'.

This scene is identical to the previous picture, but the backscene has changed from plain blue to a painted impression of dark green trees. It is beginning to look more realistic because the forest looks denser.

CHAPTER TEN

BUILDINGS

There is a huge variety of buildings available for modellers of European railways.

It is now possible to buy many types of buildings and accessories in kit or ready-assembled form in most of the popular scales. Modellers are fortunate to have such a good available selection of buildings. It is worth obtaining a few manufacturers' catalogues to become acquainted with the enormous variety of buildings and accessories. The buildings include station buildings, chalets, town houses, greenhouses, industrial premises, station overall roofs, railway structures, warehouses, tunnel mouths and so on, with most manufacturers releasing new building kits annually.

For the scratch-builder, Wills plastic sheets are retailed in OO/HO scale, but in the interests of scale a scratch-builder may choose sheets of the European (plastic and timber) sheets by various manufacturers. Again, catalogues need to be consulted. Balsa wood is useful for timber buildings and can be scribed easily. Often there are spare parts left over from kits that can be used for modification or kit-bashing purposes.

PLASTIC KITS

Busch, Faller, Heljan, Kibri, Piko, Pola and others manufacture plastic kits. Kibri, for example, retails building kits in HO, N and Z gauges. Faller is a familiar plastic-kit manufacturer and in addition to its usual ranges of buildings releases exclusive models each year that include car showrooms with revolving turntables, a fire station with a working clock and electronic fire siren, windmills, fairground rides and attractions and balloons. The Faller HO Car system features buses, lorries, coaches and so on, travelling along special roadways.

A huge coal mine made using laser-cut card was displayed on the Trix stand at the Nuremberg Toy Fair a few years ago.

The roofing on these buildings is Redutex sheets, which are available in the UK. The sheets are sold in a number of patterns and colours and are ideal for scratch-building structures for European layouts.

This O-scale station building on a Lenz demonstration layout features chimney sweeps on the roof. It is not often that this is modelled!

In addition to buildings in the popular scales, Pola building kits include G scale. Piko retails building kits in N, HO and G scales. Some of their kits are weatherproof and thus suitable for outdoor use. MKD plastic kits feature French architectural styles.

Auhagen has a good range of plastic moulded industrial building bits and pieces, including machinery, pipes, brackets, and brick-wall panels in a number of colours. These parts form part of a comprehensive integrated modular building system.

Kits that are built straight from the box do not make the most realistic models. Painting and weathering not only improves the look of a building, but it also ensures the individuality of a finished model. Acrylic or enamel paints will remove the plastic appearance of the model and it is generally best to paint the various parts before construction.

ABOVE: *A DHL logistics depot built from a Faller plastic kit. This type of 'generic' modern building could be seen almost anywhere in Europe.*

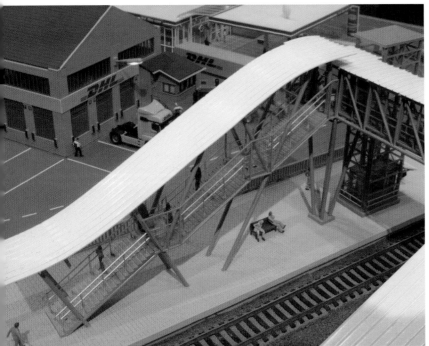

LEFT: *A modern station footbridge by Faller in HO scale as released in 2014.*

RIGHT: *Auhagen produces a good choice of modular industrial building parts. These can be used flexibly, but have still to reach the eyes of many modellers in the UK.*

BOTTOM RIGHT: *A Faller quarry structure could provide an ideal corner filler on a layout.*

Plastic kits are arguably the traditional way of making models of European buildings and, if nicely made and well painted, they can be a good source of buildings for a European layout. If you have not built a plastic kit before, a suggestion would be to build something small rather than attempting to make a complicated kit. Do not skip reading the instructions of a kit, even if it is a simple one, because some parts do have just one right way of being assembled and if you get that wrong you may not be able to finish making the kit. On some kits there are part numbers on the plastic sprue that links the different pieces. Look at these and compare them with the drawings in the instructions so as to become familiar with the kit.

Before assembly, it is worth looking at the parts that you think need painting whilst they are still on the sprue, although some parts might be best left unpainted until after assembly. Many modellers now use acrylic paints because they can easily be obtained from a number of sources, including art shops, model shops, WH Smith and Hobbycraft. These paints are water-based and once the paint has dried assembly can begin.

Carefully cut each of the pieces off the sprue with a sharp craft knife. Cut as close to the part as you can and use wet and dry paper to rub down any rough edges on the part. There are a large number of plastic adhesives on the market. For example, it is worth visiting www.deluxematerials.co.uk to see the large selection of adhesives that are available. It is worth

It is a good idea to paint the parts of a plastic kit before assembly. Kits that are assembled without painting always look 'plasticky'. This farmhouse by Kibri will be blended into the landscape on the author's next Swiss layout, complete with its adjoining vegetable garden.

buying several types of plastic cement/liquid to decide which suits your modelling style the best.

TIMBER KITS

The FidesPress range of wooden building kits is a welcome change from the familiar plastic kits and these can be painted with acrylics or stained. The FidesPress range includes Swiss and Scandinavian models in Z, O, HO and N gauges, with reasonable prices and including details supplied such as white-metal castings, signs, glazing and so on. Station buildings available include Celerina, Rueun and Saanenmöser. Some of the kits are pre-cut, with others having a cutting outline printed on to wood, leaving the builder to make the final cuts. These kits are fun to build and are a little more challenging than the usual plastic models and I have found the final result is strong and rewarding.

The Fides range of building kits also uses a mixture of laser-cut timber and card components. Other companies that make laser-cut kits include Busch, Faller and Noch. In addition, white-metal accessories are included in some kits, together with plastic glazing sheets. Each kit has full assembly diagrams, plus several building tips in English in its accompanying leaflet.

The component parts of these kits include laser-cut timber, card, photo card, metal and other accessories. These kits do require a range of skills, as well as a variety of adhesives, primer and setting times.

A small goods shed made from sheets of laser-cut timber with plastic windows left over from other projects. The walls were strengthened internally to stop them warping by using spare pieces of the laser-cut timber. I used UHU Holz Leim adhesive to assemble the model, because it is fast drying and is recommended for working with laser-cut card and timber.

Here is the goods shed again, but now painted with acrylics. The posters on the side were taken from a BLS railway leaflet and the piles of logs were made from twigs found in the author's garden.

RESIN BUILDINGS

As many modellers in the UK will know, ready-assembled buildings made from polyresin are a great way to make a village or a station quickly, because these buildings do not require painting or assembly. This type of building is still taking time to catch on in Europe, though some resin-based buildings are available from a number of companies, including Hornby International and Liliput. Some of Bachmann's Scenecraft range in both N and HO/OO scales, such as the cement works, would look equally at home on a European layout. The buildings can be used straight out of the box, or can be personalized in small ways such as adding an extension on to them, weathering the building, adding lights to the interior and attaching creeping ivy to the walls.

Though resin buildings are very popular in the UK, they are still in their infancy in Europe. Hornby International and Liliput produce a limited selection of these buildings, but most European modellers seem to prefer assembling kits rather than buying ready-finished buildings at this time. Illustrated is a permanent-way hut by Hornby International, ready-coloured and made from resin.

ALPINE BUILDINGS

Many European buildings feature timber on their external walls. Chalets in Austria, Germany and Switzerland immediately spring to mind, but many older buildings in France and Germany feature half-timbered walls. The colour of the timber will depend upon the area modelled and the age of the building. Some of the timber parts in plastic kits are moulded in light brown plastic, but on the prototype this colour is normally only seen on newly built houses and chalets, because with the passing of years timber darkens. In my experience, model buildings with darker timber look a little better, but study prototype pictures of your chosen area to see what the 'real thing' looks like. It is quite an easy task to darken the colour of the timber using acrylic paint or weathering dyes.

Window boxes are essential on most chalets in Alpine areas such as Austria, France, southern Germany, northern Italy and Switzerland. In HO and the smaller scales it is not necessary to make the boxes and then add the flowers, because a dab of white PVA woodworking glue at the base of the window or along the top of a balcony, then a sprinkling of a mixture of finely chopped-up foam in different colours is all that is required. The lack of a window box will not be noticeable, because in real life tumbling flowers would hide it anyway.

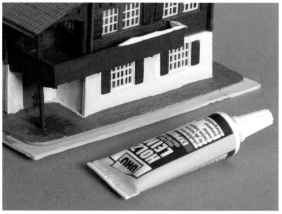

ABOVE LEFT: A nearly finished typical Alpine chalet before final detailing. I usually paint the timbers quite darkly to represent aged wood. The chalet looks in need of some flowers on the balcony timber.

ABOVE RIGHT: Quick-drying adhesive (Busch Laser Cut Glue is suitable) has been 'painted' on the top of the balcony. You need to work quite quickly because scatter material has to be sprinkled on to the adhesive before the glue begins to set.

LEFT: Close-up of the 'planted' flowers around the balcony of the chalet. A simple task that takes five minutes and only costs pence, but makes a huge visual difference.

The window on a laser-cut house looks good, but could be even better if a few flowers were added.

Just a little glue and some coloured fine scatter and the window looks more complete for a European house.

PROJECT ONE: A MODERN SBB PLATFORM SHELTER BY FIDES – A MIXED COMPONENT KIT

Kits that use a variety of materials can give excellent final results, though they do seem to cost a little more than plastic kits and they are not the most suitable kits for new recruits to the hobby because they do require a varied range of skills, involving a number of adhesives, primer, cutting techniques and setting times. The Swiss company Fides produces a

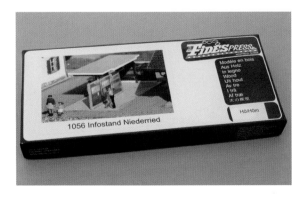

The following pictures show how to build a mixed-component kit. The FidesPress kit retails for around £25 plus post and packing from www.hobby-shop.ch.

range of mixed-material building kits and accessories in a number of scales.

I built an SBB modern platform shelter by Fides to experiment with one of these kits. It consisted of mixed components, including wood, white metal, brass, metal and photographic paper. The prototype of the platform shelter is at the Zentralbahn metre-gauge station of Niederried on Lake Brienz. I found that it took a little longer to build this kit than a plastic kit, simply because one has to use various painting and assembly techniques. Some of the parts are metal, so it is therefore necessary to prime these parts before assembly, which increases the assembly and drying time while building the kit.

I made the structure on a standalone section of thick cardboard, so when I fix the shelter to the layout I will 'drop' the cardboard into a hole in the platform. It took about three hours to make this simple kit in total, excluding the drying time of the primer, adhesives and paint. I found the supplied pictorial instructions were easy to follow and I was very pleased with the final result of the kit, which is Fides stock number 1056 and available from www.hobby-shop.ch at around £25 (early 2015 price).

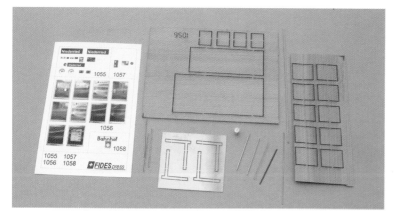

This is part of the mixed selection of parts that come with Fides kit 1056. The components include wood, white-metal detailing parts, brass, metal and signs on photographic paper.

A few of the tools required include track cutters, a micro-paintbrush, a small file and primer for the metal parts.

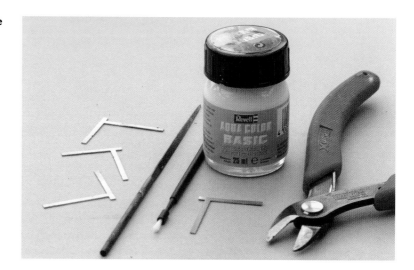

The supports for the canopy are made from the brass central support, with additional L-shaped metal pieces along the top edge that need to be fixed to the brass section with superglue. The brass pieces shown in the picture have received a first coat of primer.

I fixed the base section to a much thicker piece of cardboard to give it some extra support. Also seen are the roof section with supports in place and the semi-gloss photos cut to the right size and their edges carefully 'painted' using a black felt-tip pen.

This larger than life picture shows the finished platform canopy, which is now ready to be positioned on a layout.

The prototype for this station shelter is at the Zentralbahn station of Niederried on Lake Brienz in the Bernese Oberland area of Switzerland, which is dwarfed by the main station building.

The rear of the platform canopy at Niederried where the narrow-gauge (metre-gauge) Zentralbahn runs.

At Bowil station in the Emmental area of Switzerland (on the line between Luzern and Langnau), we see an example of this type of platform shelter on a standard-gauge line.

Top tips for working with mixed-component kits:

- These kits are not so good for first-time kit builders; plastic kits are recommended for them.
- More additional materials and tools are required when making mixed-material kits such as priming paint and metal cutters.
- Additional skills will also be needed because some of the kits include metal parts, so knowledge of cutting metal, soldering, priming and painting metal and so on will be required.

The following tools and materials will be needed:

- sharp craft knife with spare blades to cut out the signs
- resealable cutting board
- steel ruler for cutting out the signs
- small paint brushes for painting primer and the paint
- primer for painting the metal parts
- acrylic and enamel paints after the metal has been primed
- felt-tip pens to colour the edge of the cut photographic paper
- contact adhesive or superglue for assembly of the kit

- small pair of tweezers for handling the detailing parts and signs
- possibly a soldering iron instead of superglue
- metal cutters for cutting the metal parts from their backing sheet.

PROJECT TWO: A PLATFORM SHELTER BY FALLER – A LASER-CUT KIT

Laser-cut card is one of the newer materials being used for buildings, fencing, bridges, windows, doors, plants and vegetables. Laser-cut card vegetables and bridges show that this material can be both delicate and strong. Laser-cut thin card plants include ferns, reeds, water lilies, bean sticks and cabbages, and are made by ER Décor, Model Scene and Noch.

Aku, Busch, Joswood, Faller, Fides, Noch and Tip Top Modell are just some of the European companies producing building kits using laser-cut card. Trix introduced a range of large building kits, including a car factory, warehouses and a coal mine. The Busch and Noch ranges of building kits are of both large and small structures, including garden sheds and kiosks.

One of the smaller station kits by Faller is a small wayside timber-built platform waiting shelter that measures 77 × 60 × 54mm. The parts are

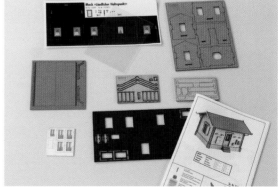

*ABOVE LEFT: **The following series of pictures demonstrates the assembly of a laser-cut kit using timber and card parts by Faller.***

*ABOVE RIGHT: **The instructions for the kit are mainly pictorial and all of the parts of this kit are laid out in this picture. A sheet of plastic is supplied to represent glass in the windows and there is also a paper insert that needs to be folded up inside the nearly finished model to supply the look of curtains in the windows.***

predominantly card, but also include thin timber, plastic, paper and clear plastic (for the windows). The laser-cut card and timber parts are held into the backing sheets by small 'tag' pieces that need to be carefully removed before assembly of the kit can begin. The pieces can be very cleanly cut out of the backing sheets if you use a craft knife with a new blade.

Assembly of the kit is in two stages – first, the inner walls are assembled, then the laser-cut timber pieces are overlaid on the inner walls. After the windows have been added to the interior of the building, the curtains need to be added by folding the paper insert and then pushing it gently inside the building. Next, the guttering, the shutters and detailing pieces can be added. After I had finished the kit, I added a station sign made on my computer.

This is a very good kit for a first-time laser-cut kit builder. It is easy to assemble and once complete looks very realistic. I found the mainly pictorial instructions to be very good and it took about two hours to make this kit, excluding the drying time of the adhesives and paint. The kit is Faller stock number 110089 and costs around £25. It is available from all Faller retailers (www.faller.de), such as Gaugemaster or Golden Valley Hobbies.

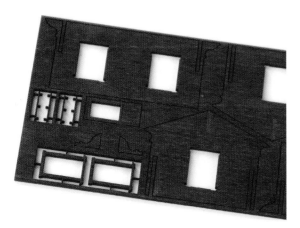

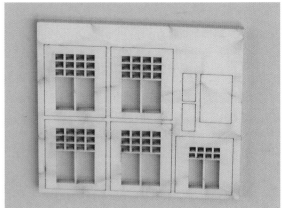

ABOVE LEFT: This close-up of the piece of laser-cut timber shows that each piece is held on to the backing sheet with several 'tags'. These can be cut through easily using a sharp craft knife over a self-sealing cutting board.

ABOVE RIGHT: The window frames also need to be removed from the backing sheet using a sharp craft knife.

ABOVE LEFT: The main walls of the building have been fitted together with the base. The front steps await assembly.

ABOVE RIGHT: Several of the laser-cut timber pieces have now been removed from the backing sheet and will need to be fixed on top of the thick cardboard sides. The assembled steps are in the lower left of the picture.

ABOVE LEFT: **The laser-cut timber sides are added as 'overlaps' on each wall. Quick-drying PVA-based adhesive has been spread on the inner wall before the outer wall is 'pushed into' the adhesive.**

ABOVE RIGHT: **Next, the windows frames need to be fitted one by one.**

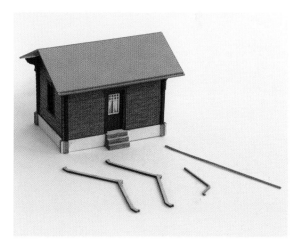

ABOVE LEFT: **The inner paper shell is folded and glued, then carefully pushed inside the building. Just be careful to line up the curtains correctly.**

ABOVE RIGHT: **The plastic guttering and roof-capping pieces need to be added next.**

LEFT: **The finished building, complete with a Swiss SBB-style sign made on a PC. I was very pleased with the end result of this building, which was a pleasure to make.**

Top tips for working with laser-cut card kits:

- All the card sections are usually carried on backing sheets, with the parts being held with small tags that need to be removed before the parts can be used.
- Always use a steel ruler and a self-sealing cutting mat; this applies even if you are only cutting through 'nicks' of card to separate the pieces from the backing card. The steel ruler directs the cutting strokes more positively and the self-sealing cutting mat protects the surface below. Only use new blades when working with laser-cut card, because blades that are tired may leave torn edges and require more cutting strokes.
- Busch Laser Cut Kleber, Deluxe Materials Roket Card Glue or UHU Holz Leim are all good for working with laser-cut card kits because they have a short drying time. If you do get excess glue on to the kit as it is being assembled, remove it with a damp cloth as quickly as possible. If the adhesive is left to dry it will result in a shiny mark on the finished building.
- Felt-tip pens, weathering dyes or a thin wash of acrylic paint can be used to colour and hide any exposed corners and joints of the laser-cut card once the kit is assembled.

LEFT: *Noch has extended its factory in Germany to produce more laser-cut kits. Here is one of its town houses using mitred card at the corners of the main walls. Light weathering to the roof and the addition of the flowers at the windows were the only changes made to the kit. To the right is an outside toilet block as one of the simpler kits in Noch's laser-cut range.*

BELOW: *Roco produces a laser-cut model of the Austrian station of Mariazell to complement its HOe-scale rolling stock.*

European kit manufacturers introduce yet more laser-cut kits made from card and wood each year. These kits are not only fun to build, but also look very realistic on completion. Here are a few sample pieces of laser-cut timber parts by Faller.

The following tools and materials will be needed:

- craft knife with spare blades for cutting the pieces from the backing sheets
- self-sealing cutting mat
- steel ruler to ensure that clean cuts are made
- small paint brushes for painting the cut edges, or precisely applying the adhesive
- acrylic paints for touching up cut edges
- felt-tip pens for touching up the edges of the card as necessary
- faster setting adhesives such as Busch Laser Cut Kleber, Deluxe Materials Roket Card Glue or UHU Holz Leim
- small pair of tweezers for handling the small parts.

PROJECT THREE: A LOW-RELIEF BACKGROUND BUILDING BY NOCH – A CD-BASED KIT

Low-relief background buildings can be made quickly using a photo-based kit and pictures. For example, Noch produces such a kit in conjunction with the German backscene manufacturer JOWI. The kit comprises a CD with images of buildings in HO, TT, N and Z scales, with eight to eleven different buildings on each CD both in jpeg and PDF format to be printed on a home colour printer. Four different CDs are available: urban landscape; old town houses; Alpine houses; and industrial buildings. Once the CD is purchased, the buildings can be printed off time and again in any of the supplied scales. The buildings depicted are modern and post-war. The pack includes ten sheets of good-quality A4 card. When the pack of ten thin cardboard sheets is exhausted, you can use similar card available from stationery shops. After printing, the buildings can be cut out using a sharp craft knife over a cutting board. I fixed the walls to 3mm cardboard using a glue stick.

These low-relief buildings are suited to kit-bashing and 'mix and match', and when fixed to strong card or foam board their potential is excellent. Using a number of differing scales of buildings on a layout introduces a 'forced perspective' appearance, making the layout look larger and deeper than it actually is. Because the sheets are effectively photographs of real buildings they can look very realistic. There is no relief on the buildings, but if some is required it would be easy to add window sills, door frames and so on by using thin cardboard.

An expanding selection of these downloadable buildings is available from: www.modellbahn-hintergrund.de.

The following series of pictures shows how to use pictures of buildings printed on paper to make low-relief buildings. This is the Noch product as it comes, with a CD plus ten pieces of high-quality thin cardboard.

The CD was loaded into a PC or a laptop.

A selection of printed buildings in HO, TT, N and Z scales.

I stuck the printed sheets on to 2mm thick cardboard using a glue stick. Be careful to rub the glue stick right to the edges of the picture to be fixed to the cardboard.

LEFT: *I supported the corners of the walls used triangular sections of thick cardboard fixed with Deluxe Materials Roket Card Glue.*

BELOW: *Here is the finished building in situ. The front is just a photograph and on closer examination there is no relief at all. The building is located between two resin buildings.*

TOP TIPS FOR BUILDINGS

- Curtains or blinds can be made from scraps of different-coloured paper, thin card or tissue. PVA adhesive or sticky tape can be used to fix the curtains in place inside the building.
- Windows can be made to look dirty by scrubbing them with sandpaper, or painting them with thinned watercolours.
- Cutting the windows with a sharp craft knife or a screwdriver can give the appearance of broken window panes.
- One way of personalizing industrial, office or station buildings is to fix signs and posters to them. Various companies sell miniature signs and posters in popular scales. Or why not make your own signs using a digital camera and a printer?
- Use Hornby's Skale Lighting system or Woodland Scenics Just Plug lighting products to add interior lights to a building. These lighting parts are suitable for most sizes of building, from Z scale through to O scale or larger.
- The visual impact of a nicely finished building can be spoilt if there is a small gap running along the lower edge of the building. One of the most important finishing touches is to 'plant' our buildings into the ground, rather than on top of the ground. PVA adhesive can be used to fix the buildings to the layout and as the glue is drying around the base of the building it is easy to sprinkle on a very fine scatter material such as Treemendus Earth powder or Woodland Scenics Fine Turf. The scatter material sticks to the drying PVA and hides the join.

EURO-MODELLING INTERLUDE – CAVALATA

An HOm layout based on the Rhätische Bahn built by professional model maker Stephan Kraus.

German professional layout builder Stephan Kraus has been engaged by various companies to produce layouts for demonstrations at model shows in Germany and other countries. His layouts look superbly realistic and the trains run very well too. Stephan's company, SMK model construction, specializes in the design and construction of high-quality, landscape-oriented model railway layouts and dioramas for commercial and private customers. Services offered range from planning a layout through to the complete implementation of 'model railway dreams'. Stephan believes that the landscape and the rails belong together and his approach is based on a 'less is more' theme, because in reality the landscape was there first and much, much later came the railway.

Stephan has been modelling since he was a boy and he was fascinated by railways and their technology, but while studying architecture at university he was drawn to modelling buildings and the variety to be seen in landscapes. He has been modelling landscapes for around thirty years and his favourite aspect is to compress real landscapes into different types of scenery, so that the viewer gets the feeling of 'almost reality'. Stephan makes his landscapes almost exclusively from expanded polystyrene, with rocks being made from moulding plaster. The buildings and the structures, including the bridges, are usually made from cardboard, polystyrene and in some cases resin.

This project illustrated here took Stephan eleven months to build, spending 724 hours in total to make it. There are about ninety trees on the layout, which were all handmade and requiring on average twenty minutes per tree to build. The layout is built on four baseboards and its trains are controlled by laptop. The topography of the layout is dominated by a wide valley, with a small station located on the front edge of the baseboard. The layout follows the familiar design of Rhätische Bahn. In the background a stone arch viaduct spans a stream and a road that leads to the station. The track plan extends over three levels and the single track ends in a loop. Two sets of hidden

Cavalata station as built by SMK model construction. The company specializes in the design and construction of high-quality, landscape-oriented model railway layouts and dioramas for commercial and private customers. SMK offers a range of services from planning a layout through to the complete implementation of 'model railway dreams'. STEPHAN KRAUS

The layout is set in springtime judging from the wild flowers in the field and the blossom on the tree.
STEPHAN KRAUS

Blue-liveried RhB crocodile passes beneath a rail-built show protection fence. STEPHAN KRAUS

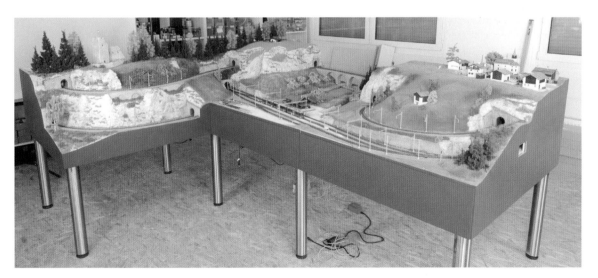

Cavalata is an L-shaped layout measuring 3.25 × 2.40m. The topography of the layout is dominated by a wide valley with a small station located on the front edge of the baseboard. The layout follows the familiar design of the RhB. In the background, a stone-arch viaduct spans both a stream and a road that leads to the station. The trackbed at a steep shoulder of the mountain descends on the left side of the layout. The track plan extends over three levels and the single track ends in a loop. Two sets of hidden sidings are designed for varied train operation and along the front edge of the system there is also a connection point for Train Safe storage tubes.
STEPHAN KRAUS

OPPOSITE PAGE: *This project for a UK customer took Stephan eleven months to build, spending 724 hours to make it in total. There are about ninety trees on the layout, which were all handmade and requiring on average twenty minutes per tree to make. The layout is built on four baseboards and its trains are controlled by laptop.* STEPHAN KRAUS

RIGHT: *The layout incorporates extensive use of static grass fibres. The technique is used judiciously so that some areas of grass are very 'patchy'.* STEPHAN KRAUS

The Glacier Express heads towards the camera. These carriages are fitted with passengers, which is essential because of the extensive areas of glass in the carriages. STEPHAN KRAUS

Blowing an Alpine horn is very much a Swiss tradition. *STEPHAN KRAUS*

sidings are designed for varied train operation and along the front edge of the system there is also a connection point for Train Safe storage tubes.

There are various scenes dotted about the layout, including railway photographers, groups of people chatting at the station, permanent-way workers and a small herd of deer near the top of the mountainside. We would like to say thank you to the UK client who has agreed that this superb layout can be featured in this book. You have a model railway to be proud of, sir!

In addition, Stephan hosts seminars demonstrating a variety of techniques, including landscape construction, making rocks, trees and weathering. The seminars are between one and two and a half days in length. No prior knowledge is required for the participation in the seminars. Stephan is happy to be contacted to discuss working on projects for clients in Europe or the UK. His website (www. modellbau-smk.de) features other layouts and dioramas, with pictures that are inspirational if you are a fan of model railways.

CHAPTER ELEVEN

DETAILING THE LAYOUT

Modellers are spoilt for choice, with an enormous range of detailing parts available.

Many people find that detailing a layout is one of the fun parts of railway modelling and so are prepared to spend a lot of time doing it. The number of details that can be added to European layouts in part depends upon the money that you wish to spend adding them to your layout. The location and time period of a layout will affect the number of details required, so, for example, a station in a rural location in the late 1960s would not require as many figures, taxis and road vehicles, or as much luggage, signage and lighting, as a model of busy Stuttgart Hbf in 2015.

Rural locations might simply need fencing, some cattle, a few trees and telegraph poles, but in contrast a busy suburban line may require road bridges, retaining walls, streetlights, pavements, lots of figures, signal gantries, road vehicles, traffic signs, graffiti and so on.

ADDING FIGURES

Figures are available in all the common scales in every imaginable pose, with some coming ready painted while others are not. It is generally best to position the figures so that they look like they are doing something, such as groups of teenagers chatting or workers in a goods yard in action poses unloading a wagon or lorry. Maybe we should buy a few seated passengers and fit them in our carriages?

Companies that make model figures for European layouts include Busch, Faller, Merten, Noch, Preiser, Vollmer and Woodland Scenics. Noch has an HO-scale range of country-specific railway officials for Austria, the Czech Republic, Denmark, France, Italy, Germany, the Netherlands, Spain, Switzerland and the UK. The figures relate to the period before dayglo jackets and privatized uniforms, so they are useful for the end of steam and the first part of the modern-image years. In addition, these companies retail policemen and postmen specifically for Austria, Germany and Switzerland with the correct uniforms and logos. Some of these recently introduced figures now have tiny LEDs.

Noch has a range of classic motorbikes in HO scale. The range includes a Norton Commando 850 and BMW R60 with sidecar. The bikes are nicely detailed with individual spokes on the wheels.

ABOVE: A busy city road scene calls for numerous figures. This scene was on the Preiser stand at the Nuremberg Toy Fair.

LEFT: Nicely painted and posed O-scale figures create an impression of real-life action. Figures can either be fixed permanently to a layout using contact adhesive, superglue or PVA, or fixed temporarily with tacky adhesive.

ABOVE: A snow scene with some very well wrapped-up HO figures by Preiser. For those modelling winter scenes, there are figures available who are skiing or snowboarding, as well as snowmen and more.

ABOVE: A selection of waiting HO-scale passengers by Preiser, including the luggage and the seat. A quick scan of the Noch and Preiser catalogues will reveal the huge number of ready-painted figures that are available for every occasion.

LEFT: Noch retails scooters with working front and rear light, plus photographers with flashing cameras for HO scale. At the 2015 Nuremberg Toy Fair it introduced N- and TT-scale figures with LED lights too.

LEFT: *A cameo scene involving an SNCF Fret Bo-Bo locomotive, plus figures by Noch and Preiser. Small scenes like this can contribute to the visual appeal of a layout.*

BELOW LEFT: **This picture of part of a signal box on an O-scale layout shows the level of detail that is possible for the larger scales.**

Figures can be fixed down to the layout with a blob of PVA adhesive, or Deluxe Materials Tacky Wax if they are to be positioned temporarily. Woodland Scenics retails Scenic Accents as a no-drip glue that allows for figure repositioning without reapplying the adhesive.

GIVING YOUR STATION AN IDENTITY

There are many products available to make a good representation of most European stations and in fact whilst doing the research for this section of the book I came across even more products than I knew existed. As with all these aspects of modelling railways it is often a matter of knowing 'who makes what' and what is available. While the big-name scenic companies make a huge range of detailing parts, each country has its own 'cottage industry', which becomes apparent the more research you do.

When a station is intended to represent a specific railway company or an area it is the small details that go a long way to setting that location. Posters and signage on the station fencing and buildings help to define the time period that the station is intended to represent. If you are modelling the current era, advertising hoardings, posters and general station posters can be made to measure by taking digital pictures of the posters you want on your layout, then reducing them to scale on screen and printing them on a colour printer. Another method is to collect various leaflets and pocket timetables, then cut these up to the size you need. I picked up one railway excursion leaflet that contained a selection of miniature station posters that were ideal for cutting out (use a sharp craft knife, steel ruler and cutting board) and sticking (glue stick) on to a piece of thin mounting card for posters at stations. Of course, if you are modelling an historical period what is suggested here is not possible. There are many accessory companies offering vintage scale posters and signage. Members of the society of your country of choice will be able to direct you to these companies.

Train destination boards and railway clocks are different in every country. This picture was taken at Geneva main station, showing the world-famous Swiss railway clock.

ABOVE LEFT: **When visiting a railway station, see what leaflets and brochures are available. These can be very useful for signs, posters and so on in miniature.**

ABOVE RIGHT: **When looking around for hoardings and posters for a layout, it is always worth studying packaging from foodstuffs and other goods. Here, cardboard boxes for biscuits and coffee are a good way to obtain well-printed signs for a layout.**

Since the mobile telephone has become popular there are fewer telephone boxes on stations, but modern telephone boxes are still a common sight at the main stations, although in reduced numbers. German company Brawa produces a good range of different telephone boxes in N and HO scales, with some boxes being illuminated. They are nicely modelled with clear plastic windows and excellent interior detail. The company also retails a good number of working station lights and station clocks for different countries.

The modern grey block-paved platform surface seen on some of the refurbished European stations can be modelled by using plastic sections from Brawa (stock number 2845), along with the upright concrete platform walling sections (stock number 2869). Faller and Noch produce flexible platform sides too.

ABOVE LEFT: **At most stations in Switzerland there is a Swisscom telephone box, although fewer of them are needed now because of the extensive use of mobile telephones by passengers.**

ABOVE RIGHT: **In HO scale, Brawa makes a model of the Swisscom telephone box with working lights. Other telephone boxes are available from Brawa in HO scale, including numerous styles of German telephone boxes and a traditional UK-style red box.**

Kibri's platform accessories kit (stock number 8108) includes ticket machines, seats, lights and other platform furniture that are pretty generic in style and can be painted in the railway colours of your chosen location. Rietze (www.rietze.de) produces a number of station accessories such as bus stops, vending machines and Automat ticket machines, which are a good way to increase the location identity of a station.

Increasingly, 'cottage industry' firms are making kits of station buildings of laser-cut timber construction. These are not as cheap as mass-produced plastic kits, but are generally superb and enable a model of a specific location to be built.

One non-railway item that can really set the location of a station is a local bus, a postbus or a touring coach, because many bus and postbus timetables in Europe sensibly connect with rail timetables such that no European station forecourt will be complete without at least one bus or coach. Rietze makes model road vehicles and is one of the world's largest manufacturers of coaches and buses in HO scale. Every few months, the company produces a specials leaflet that can be viewed on its website, with a range that includes ambulances, cars, vans, police vehicles, local buses and postbuses for countries including Austria, France, Germany and Switzerland. Forklift trucks for station platforms are available from Wiking and there is a huge number of cars, buses, vans and coaches produced by Brekina, Busch, Faller, Herpa, Rietze, Schuco, Wiking and more. Some of these road vehicles include emergency vehicles with flashing lights and others with working head and tail lights.

RIGHT: Ticket machine on station platform. Details such as these are often made by local specialist suppliers and one of the challenges when modelling a European railway system is to become aware of such suppliers. Buying a model railway magazine of that country and visiting a local model railway show are two ways of doing this.

BELOW: The familiar 'Do Not Cross' sign at all Swiss stations. Some 'cottage industry' firms in Switzerland make models of these signs, or they can be made based on your own digital photographs.

A BLS track-maintenance crew delivering a 'Do Not Cross' sign (made from part of a photo taken on a digital camera printed on a home printer) on a Robel Tm 235 track-maintenance unit that is available from Kibri in HO as a made-up model.

Look through modelling magazines of your chosen country and you will soon come across adverts of smaller manufacturers that produce what you need for your station. For example, in Switzerland Microscale makes a good range of detail accessories, including station, advertising boards, illuminated station signs and 'Do Not Cross' notices. In addition, it produces signals in N and HO scales and other accessories (www.microscale.ch).

ACCESSORIES

Newcomers to European railway modelling will be surprised at the vast range of scenic accessories that is readily available. Listed here are just some of the main manufacturers to provide a flavour of what is available. Beli-Beco, Brawa, Busch, Faller, Noch, Schneider and others retail miniature lighting. Viessmann produces model gas lamps in Z, N, HO and G scales. Flashing beacons, road-up signs, advertising hoardings and garden-party fairy lights are just some of the selection of 'fun' scenic possibilities from these European manufacturers. Increasingly,

there are electronically activated men cutting wood, cows eating grass and so on from Viessmann and others.

Busch has a good road-maintenance range, including snowploughs, highway depots and their accessories. Many of its building kits use laser-cut technology. One recent theme to its new releases was a paper mill with a gatehouse, factory, warehouse, paper rolls and cellulose bales, as well as a matching narrow-gauge locomotive with wagons, vans, trucks and excavators.

Faller produces a working road system, enabling the vehicles to move along and the front wheels to turn. These are certainly an eye-catching feature at model railway exhibitions. For more information go to www.faller.de.

Kibri has various buildings with LED working lights, including a modern bus station and a station incorporating a parade of shops. There is a selection of catenary installation rail vehicles, plus road vehicles with lights. Most of these are in HO scale, but for N scale a recent introduction was a windmill with moving sails.

Every year, Noch introduces a huge number of new items. Its theme for 2015 is 'Right and Left along the Tracks', with lots more laser-cut building and detailing kits. It has new painted figures, plus unpainted figure kits, and in TT and N scale figures have been introduced with LED lighting effects. There is also a treehouse in a tree in HO/OO scale. Culverts are made from hard foam and rust-effect paint is introduced. There are also various buildings that include moving parts and lights, including a level crossing and loco shed doors, plus a Film Festival screen. The range of trees has been expanded, with tree kits, Mediterranean trees and apple trees for orchards. Foliage mats have been improved and an arable field is available. Noch also announced a new layout-making guidebook in English, together with the introduction of 3-D details. Noch offers all types of landscaped layouts for N, TT and HO scales and even Z-gauge layouts in briefcases. Noch retails road markings and surfaces, including cobbles.

Cable cars in N and HO scale for Alpine settings can be purchased from the Brawa range of accessories and scenic features. In HO scale, Brawa retails a model of the revolving Titlis cable cars in Engelberg, Switzerland. Continuing with the Alpine theme, Kibri's range of buildings includes a pack making a small village comprising a station building, church and two chalets with outbuildings. Another company that retails cable cars is Jägerndorfer, whose range is extensive and includes cable cars, skiers, snowploughs, blowers and accessories.

One European manufacturer that specializes in model viaducts, bridges and model rail/motorway soundproofing barriers is Modellbau Laggies. Kibri retails a huge variety of bridges and some manufacturers retail models of specific viaducts. For example, Faller sells a kit of the Bietschtal Viaduct on the BLS Lötschberg route in both HO and N scales. Noch produces a good number of bridge kits from laser-cut card that are surprisingly strong and look good.

For canals and waterways the products of Artitec will be useful, because it produces HO- and N-scale tugs, canal boats, launches, ferry boats, fishing vessels, crab cutters and dockside equipment in various European styles, including those based in Holland and Norway.

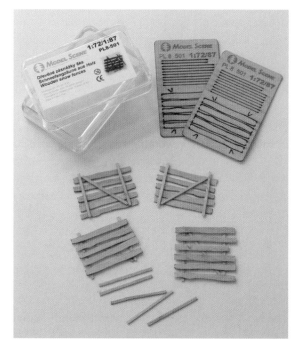

LEFT: **Wooden snow fences made from real timber are available from Model Scene. The individual pieces need to be cut from the backing piece with a sharp craft knife.**

ABOVE: **After assembly, the snow fence was lightly stained using a thin wash of acrylic dark brown paint. The fence will then be located above the railway line on a steep slope to prevent snow blocking the line.**

Busch, Faller, JOWI, MZZ, Vollmer and others retail backscenes that incorporate mountain, hillside and valley locations. The use of backscenes should not be underestimated – they add depth to a narrow layout and are another useful way of identifying the region that you wish to reproduce in miniature.

Viessmann produces a functional tamping machine and catenary-laying wagons, a pile-boring machine, modern level-crossing gates that raise and fall and a comprehensive interior lighting system.

PROJECT: MAKING A MODEL BY FALLER OF THE DB PLUSPUNKT

Following Germany's unification in 1990, the two railway systems of the former West and East Germany, Deutsche Bundesbahn (DB) and Deutsche Reichsbahn (DR), were merged. It was interesting to see the different railway trends that took place after unification, with some of the lines in the West reopening, whilst some in the former East Germany were closed because of the increase in ownership of private cars. Various independent operators, both passenger and freight, have won tenders in competition with DB and many stations throughout Germany are being modernized, using a common national corporate theme with plenty of glass, steel and red towers.

Tied in with station improvements, consideration has been given to the station environment because some had become rather derelict. With that in mind, DB set about introducing changes to improve the cleanliness, communications at stations and the safety of passengers. The larger stations attracted the greatest investment, but DB has worked hard to develop medium and smaller stations. One of the most noticeable features of the new station facilities has been the introduction of the DB Pluspunkt, which means information point, with red towers that are visible in the landscape and a variety of features, including an automatic ticket machine, a ticket-validation machine, an emergency call point, a card telephone, travel information and seating. The size of the tower and its facilities depends upon the size of the station. There are Mini, Midi and Maxi Pluspunkts using basic modules, though the size and shape vary among stations. The size of the waiting shelter with seats is determined by the importance of the station. A nearby panel displays arrival and departure timetables, together with other information notices.

The Faller Pluspunkt kit was introduced in HO scale in 2005 (stock number 120234) with three Pluspunkts: one mini, one midi and one maxi. For each, there is a red tower, an information noticeboard, a waiting shelter (two for the maxi Pluspunkt) and a waste bin. The kit comprises four large plastic sprues and a self-adhesive sheet of DB logos, timetables, station signs and other paraphernalia. There is a mainly pictorial explanatory leaflet (usefully with some English text), which shows the assembly order of the parts. Whilst it is not strictly necessary to paint the parts, I never leave a plastic kit unpainted. I find that by painting a model it adds that personal touch and increases job satisfaction and the finished model will generally look better. I used acrylic paints with various sizes of brushes and left them a few hours to dry before removing the pieces from the sprues. I found that by cutting close to the part with a sharp knife there was little surplus plastic that I needed to remove. In a few cases, I used a piece of fine sandpaper to smooth the 'nick' that was left on the part. I assembled the parts with contact adhesive, trying to be careful not to let it get on the surface of the clear plastic representing the glass, because it does quickly create 'frosted glass'.

Usefully, the supplied notices and timetables are self-adhesive. I found them to be a little fiddly to get correctly into position and on several of them I trimmed the edge to provide a better fit. On the midi Pluspunkt I painted and assembled the central red module before I affixed the posters, which are on the inside walls of the unit. That was a mistake! It was quite a job to ensure that the posters were applied vertically. I suggest that all posters, timetables and so on are best applied after painting, but before assembly of the parts. The maxi Pluspunkt has the facility for a light within the red central unit. The bulb (stock number 180671)

A modern DB passing station on the German branch line between Immenstadt and Obertsdorf, with a DB Class 612 two-car unit on 4 February 2011.

The Faller Pluspunkt kit builds three Pluspunkts: one mini, one midi and one maxi. For each there is a red tower, an information noticeboard, a waiting shelter (two for the maxi Pluspunkt) and a waste bin. The kit includes a self-adhesive sheet of DB logos, timetables, station signs and other paraphernalia.

RIGHT: *A Telekom phone box by Brawa, assembled and painted, and a waiting shelter by Kibri stand on top of a plastic platform surface by Brawa, which can also supply the platform upright walls.*

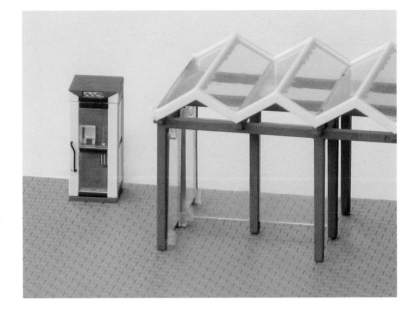

BELOW: *A detailed DB station with a DB Class 642 unit by Piko. Note the DB red Pluspunkt in the background, plus other modern waiting shelters, waste bins and accessories.*

In 2013, Faller introduced a kit for trackside noise-reduction barriers that are now seen extensively in many European countries.

is not included with the kit, but the instruction leaflet covers its possible incorporation in the model. It took me about four hours to build all three Pluspunkts.

For more information about DB Pluspunkt, just type 'DB Pluspunkt' into an Internet search engine and you will soon find photographs of the real thing. The German *MIBA* railway-modelling magazine special number 50 contains a four-page article on Pluspunkts with scale drawings (www. miba.de).

CHAPTER TWELVE

ROAD VEHICLES

Adding detailing parts improves the appearance of vehicles.

There are many companies that produce excellent models of road vehicles in various scales, with the current crop of model road vehicles being so much more realistic since the days of diecast and plastic vehicles without windows, with hard plastic wheels and poor paint finishes. Many of today's models of road vehicles have windscreen wipers, plastic light fixings, good liveries and paint finishes, nicely applied decals, door-mounted rear-view mirrors, registration plate numbers, manufacturer's badge, the correct type of wheels and more.

There is a very good selection of model road vehicles in N and HO scales with working lights to add a further dimension to road scenes on model railways.

This concrete road overbridge was seen on the Heki display layout at the Nuremberg Toy Fair. It makes a change to see a road section modelled high above a valley floor rather than a railway line on a viaduct.

In many places in Europe integrated public transport of rail and road, or rail and tram, or indeed rail and boat is frequently seen. Arguably Switzerland leads the way in this and a local postbus calls as the train arrives in the scene modelled by Stephan Kraus.

ADDING EXTERNAL DETAILS

Buses and coaches from European manufacturers often come with add-on parts such as driver's mirrors and windscreen wipers. To demonstrate how easy it is to add the additional details to a Rietze plastic model of a German local bus, an accompanying picture sequence is included here. The Rietze German local bus came with two plastic sprues of add-on parts – one set on a red plastic sprue, the other on a black plastic sprue. First, it was necessary to clean off some of the excess plastic from the plastic mirrors with a sharp craft knife. Then I pushed the mirrors into the holes above the two side windows. Once the mirror was pushed in as far as it would go, I dribbled a small blob of plastic cement around the connection.

The windscreen wipers were a little harder to fix to the vehicle because they are quite tiny. I needed to use a pair of fine-nosed tweezers to position them in the indentations just below the front windscreen. Holding the bus in the air with the wipers in place, I dribbled a spot of plastic cement into the point where the wiper attached to the coach front and waited a few seconds until I moved the coach so as to give time for the cement to fix the wiper.

This German MAN local bus by Rietze came with a pack of add-on parts. It really does call out for a driver and some passengers in the interior.

ABOVE LEFT: **One plastic sprue contained the wipers, while the other had the mirrors. The parts can be cut off using a sharp craft knife over a self-sealing cutting board.**

ABOVE RIGHT: **On the back of the bus there is an indentation for a number plate.**

ABOVE LEFT: **With Kibri road vehicle kits comes a sheet of number plates and signs. I carefully cut out number plates for the front and rear of the bus.**

ABOVE RIGHT: **Then I used a black felt-tip pen to colour the cut edges of the number plates.**

Here are the parts to add to the bus: windscreen wipers, mirrors and number plates.

ABOVE LEFT: **Using a pair of fine-nosed tweezers, I pushed the number plate into a little fast-drying white glue.**

ABOVE RIGHT: **The completed front of the bus with the added parts.**

LEFT: **The back of the bus looks a lot better now that the number plate has been added. This completed the work that took less than an hour.**

From start to finish, including adding the wipers and mirrors and the number plates, it took less than an hour. I was very pleased with adding a little individuality to the bus and I will certainly undertake similar work on other road vehicles that I buy. There are various additional projects that I now need to do on the bus, including the addition of a selection of passengers and a driver, plus a little light weathering.

ADDING INTERIOR DETAILS

To access the interior of a road vehicle the first thing is to remove the body, although in my experience the bodies of road vehicles are attached to the chassis in several different ways, so it is a matter of trial and error to get familiar with the methods used by different manufacturers. Some road vehicles are made partially from metal, whilst others are made entirely from plastic. The Rietze plastic local bus used here to demonstrate some of the techniques in the accompanying pictures came apart by removing the front and rear light plastic mouldings. The light mouldings were effectively holding the body and chassis together by means of plastic 'pins' on the reverse of the rear light modules.

The windows on some model buses and coaches are darker than on others, as in real life – some are tinted, others are not. Where the windows are tinted, you may consider that it is not worth spending time and effort detailing the interior. In my case, the side windows of the Oberland Tours coach were quite dark, so I saw little point in adding passengers, but I did consider that it was worthwhile painting the seats light blue because these would then be vaguely visible through the tinted windows. To paint the seats

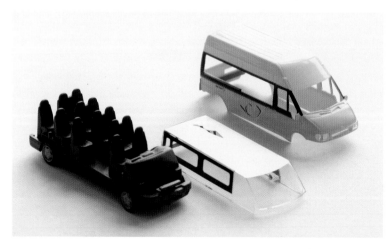

ABOVE: *I purchased this HO model of a Swiss Ford Transit postbus, but I was not happy that the line of yellow showed below the side windows.*

LEFT: *I took the model apart, which comprised the chassis with seats, the windows and the body.*

RIGHT: I painted the seats and interior that would be visible through the windows with matt paint, then the seated figures were glued to the seats with a blob of contact adhesive. There is a party atmosphere in this particular bus!

BELOW: After an hour's work the finished postbus looks more realistic and I now need to add a number plate to the vehicle.

in a bus or a coach, a small paintbrush and some acrylic paints are all that is required. It is useful if you know roughly what colour the seats would be in real life so as to make the model as prototypical as you can.

Though the side windows on the touring coach were tinted, the front screen was not, so I decided to fit a driver because the empty driver's seat would be readily visible. I looked through my stock of miniature figures and located a sitting passenger with arms outstretched as if he was driving. Some of the plastic needed to be removed with a sharp craft knife from his thighs and legs before he became a snug fit in the driver's seat. Once I was happy that the driver would be 'sitting comfortably', I positioned him in place with a tiny piece of Blu-Tack and replaced the body of the coach so that I could check if the lack of lower legs would be visible through the front screen. Fortunately they were not, so I could happily proceed to fixing the driver to his seat with a blob of plastic cement, ensuring that one of his hands was positioned to look like he was holding the steering wheel.

The following tools and materials will be needed:

- fine-nosed tweezers to handle the wipers, the mirrors and the number plates
- sharp craft knife for cutting the plastic add-on pieces from their sprues and for cutting out the number plates
- plastic cement
- small paintbrush to apply the plastic cement to fix the add-on plastic parts
- small paintbrush and light-coloured acrylic paint for the seats
- number plates from a road vehicle kit
- self-sealing cutting mat and steel ruler for cutting out the number plates
- black felt-tip pen for colouring the edges of the cut number plates
- a little fast-drying PVA-based adhesive to fix the number plates
- one seated driver and additional passenger figures (as required).

EURO-MODELLING INTERLUDE – BAHNLAND BAYERN

A DB-based HO-scale layout by Paul Smith.

This busy HO-scale layout has a river overbridge as one of its central scenic elements and I will now describe how it was made. After finalizing the track plan, the baseboards were constructed and for this layout I used an open-frame construction in order that the scene could incorporate changes in the land profile, including a river valley with a rail bridge. The trackbed was cut and adjusted for level using vertical ply risers that are attached to the cross-formers. It is important when building a layout using this technique that the track plan has been decided, as later amendments to the terrain profile to accommodate changes in track layout are more difficult than on a conventional flat-topped baseboard.

When the main structure of the baseboards was complete, the trackbed was finalized and the terrain formed using plaster bandage. For the flat areas such as road surfaces, car parks or where buildings will later be added, I used card or polystyrene core board. For the river wall along the right-hand bank, I utilized brick-embossed Plastikard. With the plaster bandage set, the river bed base colour was added using a waterproof paint (any regular artists' acrylic), before adding any items that will be set in the resin-based water. The river wall was also painted and the flat area that will form the restaurant car park was undercoated with a spray-can grey primer to seal the surface. Once the base colour had dried, the river bed was created using a mixture of sharp sand and fine stones. This was dried first on a foil-lined baking tray before setting with a waterproof PVA solution. Finally, before pouring the resin, the detail elements such as larger stones, gravel and various reeds and rushes from Noch's laser-cut range were set into the river bank.

With the basics of the river bed in place, the next element was the addition of the bridge structure. The bridge deck itself was formed of 9mm exterior plywood supported on vertical risers, the non-structural sides were from a Kibri single-track stone bridge kit (39720). The decorative sides from the kit were adapted into a larger structure suitable for a twin-track main line using embossed Plastikard to form the arches. Before securing the bridge in place, the track crossing the bridge and all power feeds were added; this included a crossover between the two running lines. The Tortoise slow-action point machines were hidden within the bridge piers and care was taken during this construction to ensure that the wiring and point machines were accessible from the underside of the layout after completion of the bridge in case of failure.

The river bank was painted and various scatter materials used to create the edges of the river, with the river itself made from Woodland Scenics E-Z Water, a pourable resin that is heated and poured in thin layers. Care was taken not to rush this stage and to allow each layer to cool between pours, or the resin will shrink from the river edges, leaving unsightly gaps, or, worse, it will crack. The river bridge was weathered and handrails added along the sides.

The timber foundations for the river bed and banks as built by Paul Smith on his Bahnland Bayern layout. PAUL SMITH

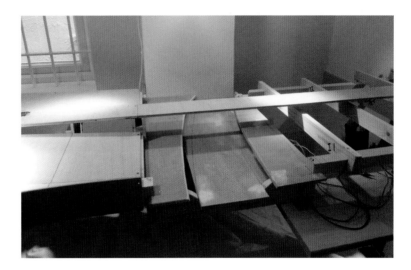

The trackbed sits on plywood and the slopes on this section of the layout have been covered with plaster cloth. PAUL SMITH

The completed river with a Voith Gravita locomotive crossing. PAUL SMITH

BAHNLAND BAYERN
LAYOUT PROFILE

Name: Bahnland Bayern

Type of layout: continuous run with seven-platform urban station and industrial sidings (a chemical works)

Era: Epoch VI–VIb

Location: south-eastern Bavaria, Germany

Scale: HO

Dimensions: overall dimensions are 5.4 × 3.9m, with the operator in the centre of the layout

Track: Tillig HO Elite Code 83 (wooden sleeper track for sidings and all turnouts), with Roco concrete sleeper track on the main line

Ballast: Woodland Scenics multiple shades fine ballast; light grey (recently laid main-line concrete sleeper track), buff, brown (for older sidings); the track and ballast were weathered using acrylic paints

Control: ESU ECoS 50200, NCE DCC point motor decoders (Switch-8/Switch-It) and Tortoise switch machines

Locomotives: ACME, Brawa, ESU, Liliput, LS Models, Mehano and Roco

Freight wagons: ACME, Brawa, Fleischmann and Roco

Coaching stock:	ACME, LS Models and Roco	**River Bridge:**	Kibri stone viaduct adapted
Landscaping:	Woodland Scenics Plaster		to double track using Slater's
	Cloth laid over hard foam		Plastikard stone sheets
	pieces; the plaster cloth was	**Buildings:**	Kibri (restaurant)
	then painted and treated with	**Trees:**	home made using floristry
	scatter materials and later		wire, plaster and Woodland
	with static grass fibres of		Scenics scatter material
	various manufacturers using a		plus others by Noch and
	Noch Gras-master		Busch
River Scene:	Woodland Scenics E-Z Water,	**Figures:**	Noch and Preiser
	sharp sand (river bed) with	**Scenic materials:**	Noch and Woodland Scenics
	Woodland Scenics stone	**Scenic details:**	Noch laser-cut plants
	chippings and Noch laser-cut	**Building time:**	the project was commenced
	reeds and bulrushes		in May 2012 and is ongoing.

Bahnland Bayern is a well-modelled layout in HO scale by Paul Smith. PAUL SMITH

The catenary and blocks of flats on Bahnland Bayern set the scene as a location in southern Germany.
PAUL SMITH

Belgian Railways SNCB locomotive and rolling stock have strayed south to Bahnland Bayern.
PAUL SMITH

CHAPTER THIRTEEN

MODELLING EUROPEAN RAIL TIMBER OPERATIONS

The extensive movement of timber by rail in Europe calls out to be modelled.

Stand on any European main-line station where freight passes through and it will soon be clear just how much timber is being transported by rail in Europe. With over one-third of the land area of the European Community covered with trees, the movement of logs, sawn timber and paper products is big business for Europe's railways.

THE FORESTRY INDUSTRY AND MOVING TIMBER BY RAIL

European forests provide a renewable natural resource, with their ecosystems being a source of food and shelter for wildlife. In addition, forests attract tourists who like outdoor pursuits and of course they supply oxygen for us all. Products derived from trees include logs, sawn timber, paper, laminates, cardboard, chipboard, plywood, bark chippings, telegraph poles, railway sleepers and much more.

The life cycle of production of commercially managed forests is plant, grow, fell, plant, grow and fell again. This cycle creates patchwork forests, with various types of trees at different stages of their development. This cycle means that felled trees and their products need to be transported.

Shunting in full swing at the small passing station as an SNCF Fret Bo-Bo locomotive moves around two loaded DB Ealos wagons.

Two ÖBB Taurus locomotives pull fifteen loaded wagons of various types filled with sawn logs away from Jenbach station on 7 October 2013.

An ÖBB standard-gauge wagon loaded with sawn logs on a narrow-gauge transporter wagon at Niedersill on the Pinzgau Bahn on 8 October 2013.

Sawmills are dotted all over Europe. Some of the mills are huge, whilst others such as this one are smaller family-run businesses.

The first wooden railway tracks carried primitive wagons pushed or pulled by humans or animals transporting stones, logs and coal. In Europe, today's railways have an important role in the movement of timber and its products. We will look briefly at rail timber operations in four European countries: Austria, France, Germany and Switzerland.

AUSTRIA

Almost half of Austria's land area is forested. At the lower levels the trees are mainly oak and beech, but above 500m these give way to beech and fir. Over 1,350m, fir trees dominate and then the higher you go, larch and pines form the majority. Commercially grown forests in mountainous areas cover 57 per cent of the land, with over a quarter of a million of Austria's population employed in the paper and timber industries.

To meet the needs of Austria's forestry and timber industry, ÖBB Rail Cargo Austria has a comprehensive transport package for the movement of timber. Timber is taken by lorry to designated ÖBB stations that have facilities for loading timber on to rail wagons. Through some of its subsidiaries specializing in the movement of timber, ÖBB offers a 'one-stop shop' for customers requiring the movement of timber by rail and road, transporting 6 million cubic metres each year within Austria and across its borders. It is central Europe's largest carrier of timber, moving around 200,000 wagons of timber each year to various economic centres in south-east Europe, including Italy, Greece, Turkey and Bosnia-Herzegovina. Annually, nearly 1 million cubic tonnes of sawn timber are loaded on around 10,000 wagons in Villach for block-train transport to the port of Koper for trans-shipment on to ships bound for the Middle East and Asia. At Villach, the train is assembled from wagons from Austria, Switzerland, Germany and Italy into block trains for onward transportation.

For moving wood chips, the Rail Cargo Group, in conjunction with Innofreight, has developed the WoodTainer XXL, of which 6,000 of these containers are now in use in Europe. These are basically open containers that can be handled by special road equipment to raise the containers and tip the wood chips out.

Another innovation is the WoodRailer wagon that can be used for carrying logs or containers. The wagons have the advantage that they can be used flexibly, with stanchions that are pivoted to withstand heavy loads and can easily be tilted down manually to facilitate either timber or container loads. These are known as the 'Rohholzbulle' (Rnooss-uz) wagons.

Working closely with the paper industry, Rail Cargo Austria AG collects cellulose from European ports and moves timber, waste paper and chemicals. The company transports half of the paper that the country exports and half of all Austria's timber products of the paper and cellulose industry. Around 3,000 different types of paper are produced in Austria.

FRANCE

The storm known as Klaus that battered southwestern France in January 2009 caused severe damage to the forests, with the result that millions of cubic metres of wood ended up available for purchase. Kronoswiss, a unit of the Swiss Krono group and a major manufacturer of wood panelling, purchased much of this wood to use at its plant at Menznau, in central Switzerland. Initially, the logs were moved in complete trains, but as volumes decreased, complete trains were no longer needed. Fret SNCF then moved single wagonloads to Kronoswiss, working with the freight forwarder Eurorail.

The Swedish paper manufacturer ScandFibre uses a single partner to transport 1.8 million tonnes of reels of paper from southern Sweden to ten European countries. Captrain, a subsidiary of SNCF, consolidates the shipments between Sweden and hubs in Hamburg and Dortmund in Germany. From there, whole trains or groups of wagons are sent to all destinations. There are now sixty trains a week carrying the traffic to ten countries: Austria, Belgium, the Czech Republic, France, Germany, Italy, Poland, Serbia, Spain and Switzerland.

GERMANY

DB Schenker Rail is the highest-volume freight carrier in the EU, with over 20,000 staff serving 4,500 customers' sidings in Germany, the Netherlands, Denmark, Italy and Switzerland and operating over 5,000 freight trains per day.

Every year, DB Schenker Rail, in partnership with the Deutsche Bahn subsidiary DB Schenker Nieten GmbH, transports around 6 million tonnes of raw and cut timber, chipboard, mature timber, pellets and wood chips through its comprehensive network of timber-loading stations and a large fleet of special freight wagons. They have developed an IT platform specifically for the timber industry and a growing number of customers use this online timber portal in Germany for ordering and to receive real-time status information. Today, DB Schenker Rail carries around 9 million tonnes of paper and pulp a year, all over Europe. Paper rolls can be carried in an upright or a horizontal position. For customers without a siding of their own, they organize access by truck via distribution warehouses.

DB Schenker has over 100,000 wagons and each year carries about 100,000 freight wagonloads of timber, 60 per cent carrying raw timber, 25 per cent carrying sawn timber and 15 per cent carrying chipboard and other goods. DB Schenker Rail has more than 6,000 freight wagons for raw timber transportation.

The most commonly used wagons are of the following types: Snps, Roos and Ea (os or nos). For timber products – such as sawn timber and chipboards – the usual wagons are two- and four-axle freight cars.

Bavaria is trying to attract more timber traffic to rail. New sidings, such as in Rosenheim, and additional loading sidings have increased the transfer to rail as the environmentally friendly means of timber transport. From 2001 to 2004, the amount of timber transported by rail increased by 25 per cent.

SWITZERLAND

In Switzerland, as with other European countries, farmers and foresters have managed Alpine forests for centuries using methods suited to the local conditions. Their forest management regime, adopted in the nineteenth century, only permits the cutting of trees that can be replaced. The Swiss forestry industry employs 90,000 people, with around 31 per cent of the country being covered in trees. In Switzerland, the main types of trees are: conifers (twelve species), 61 per cent; and broad-leaved trees (over forty species), 39 per cent. The Lothar hurricane in December 1999 destroyed 13.8 million cubic metres of forest over an area of 46,000 hectares.

Two wagons loaded with logs are headed by SBB Re 4/4 11317 at Spiez, Switzerland. Stand on any European main-line station where freight passes through and it will soon be clear just how much timber is being transported by rail. With over one-third of the land area of the European Community covered with trees, the movement of logs, sawn timber and paper products is big business on European railways.

SBB Cargo carries around 6 million tonnes of timber products, including pulp, timber, wood chippings, paper, waste paper and chemicals, every year. An example of rail involvement in the timber industry is the company of Kronospan, located in Menznau in the Canton of Lucerne, which produces chipboard and laminates and has a huge appetite for timber, much of which is transported to its premises by rail. Another example is a Swiss paper wholesaler, Sihl+Elka, which has more than doubled the amount of its paper products that it transports by rail since 1998.

SBB Cargo has about 12,000 wagons in service. The company is investing in the modernization and renewal of its fleet over the next few years and these improvements will include low-noise brake systems and special-purpose wagons. Timber is usually carried in SPS wagons.

MODELLING TIMBER OPERATIONS

ROAD VEHICLES

Road vehicles carrying logs can be obtained from a variety of sources, including Kibri's plastic kits of log-carrying vehicles. These include Mercedes Benz trailer lorries for long logs and MAN lorries with matching trailers for carrying shorter logs. These are available from www.goldenvalleyhobbies.com and other retailers in the UK.

A timber-carrying lorry with a mounted crane for loading and unloading. On this lorry the logs are well-established trees and only nine could be carried.

A log-carrying trailer with stanchions that can be raised and lowered.

MAN lorry with a trailer carrying sawn timber planks in the Simmental Valley in Switzerland.

Other European manufacturers of motor vehicles suitable for forestry locations include Busch, Rietze and Wiking. Viessmann produces moving lumberjacks and a grabber with moving parts that would add life to a timber-loading scene (www.viessmann-modell.de).

A Volvo log loader is available from Atlas in HO scale and Cararama in HO and 1:50 scale. The grabs on the vehicle can be opened and closed and the arm raised or lowered for positioning in a timber siding.

A Volvo log loader is available from Atlas in HO scale and Cararama in HO and 1:50 scale. The grabs on the vehicle can be opened and closed and the arm raised or lowered for positioning in a timber siding.

This HO-scale Unimog came with a trailer for carrying long logs. It has been weathered a little.

A plastic kit-built log-carrying Mercedes lorry and trailer by Kibri. Other European manufacturers of motor vehicles suitable for forestry locations include Busch, Rietze and Wiking.

This HO-scale log-carrying lorry was built from a Kibri kit. The vehicle has stanchions for carrying logs, plus an integral crane for loading purposes. The crane is usefully not fixed in one position.

A Herpa timber-carrying lorry with trailer and plastic logs as it comes out of the box. There is just too much shiny red plastic for my liking.

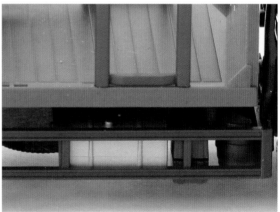

ABOVE LEFT: **To make some very simple improvements to the appearance of the lorry a little grey acrylic paint and small paintbrushes were used.**

ABOVE RIGHT: **The lower part of the stanchions with the cross-piece in red, which looks like what it is – a one-piece plastic moulding.**

LEFT: **After a few minutes' work, the cross-pieces of the stanchions have been painted grey and the stabilizers too. Both of these were previously red.**

RIGHT: *The real twigs that will be used for the load will look a lot better than the supplied plastic ones.*

BELOW: *The detailed and weathered Mercedes stake lorry by Herpa.*

RAIL WAGONS

The wagons most commonly used for the transportation of logs are:

- Eaos – open-bogie wagons that hold up to 51sq m, mainly for standard lengths of logs up to 4m
- Eanos – open-bogie wagons that hold up to 82sq m, mainly for standard lengths of logs up to 4m
- Snps – a flat-bogie wagon holding 61sq m of timber up to 19m in length. Wagons have stanchions on each side and have a robust tie-down fastening system

- Roons – for long and short wood transport, these are flat-bogie wagons with stanchions on each side, a raised bulkhead and eight tie-down fastenings. Loading of tree trunks is usually permitted without additional securing if the wood is loaded only to the height of stakes. The stanchions are movable and therefore adjustable to the lengths of the stacked logs
- Roos – are for long and short wood transport, being a flat-bogie wagon with sixteen stakes on each side, a raised bulkhead and eight tie-down fastenings.

The narrow-gauge Swiss RhB network carries large quantities of logs on its metre-gauge network.

A loaded Ros wagon at Jenbach on 7 October 2013. Shorter logs are stacked within the stakes on the wagon, with some longer lengths on the top.

SPS wagon at Salzburg 13 August 2010. The securing ropes can hardly be seen in this photograph. They run across the top of the logs through the centre of the stakes.

A recent-build Eanos bogie wagon operated by Rail Cargo Hungaria on a block train of timber at Jenbach on 7 October 2013.

ABOVE LEFT: *Securing straps holding the logs in place in a DB Ealos wagon. Straps are seen in all sorts of colours, including black, grey, red and yellow.*

ABOVE RIGHT: *Open wagons that carry logs such as this Eaos wagon get very knocked about with the constant movement of logs in and out of the wagon. One way to deform the sides of such model plastic-bodied wagons is to carefully apply a little heat to the side of the wagon and push out from the inside ever so gently. This SBB wagon was parked at Erlenbach im Simmental, Switzerland, on 8 May 2010.*

This DB Roos wagon was carrying cut timber on a mixed freight train at Salzburg on 11 May 2011.

This Rnooss-uz bogie timber wagon has five bundles of logs seen at Jenbach on 7 October 2013. The logs on this particular wagon are very much the same size and very neatly stacked.

RIGHT: This picture demonstrates that different lengths of logs can be carried on the same wagon, seen at Jenbach, Austria.

BELOW: A mixed-freight train with Eanos open wagons and Snps stake wagons both loaded with logs at Göschenen, Switzerland, on the Gotthard line.

Various models of these wagons are available, mainly in HO scale, but increasingly in N, TT and O scales too. Piko makes Roos wagons in DB liveries of a variety of eras, including DB Cargo colours. Jouef produces an SNCF Roos wagon fitted with a load of cut timber. Electrotren produces a bogie wagon complete with a load of real sawn timber. A twin timber carrying wagon is to be introduced by Liliput; these Laaps 565 wagons have seen use in Austria, France, Germany and Switzerland. Steel-sided Eaos are available in HO scale from both Roco and Liliput. Not all of these wagons are in current production, but those which are not are usually available via eBay or from second-hand dealers such as Contikits.

Sawn timber carried on a couple of ÖBB wagons.
PAUL SMITH

Sawn timber carried on an ÖBB wagon with black strapping. PAUL SMITH

Privately owned V84 shunting locomotive of the Austrian Salzburger Lokalbahn. PAUL SMITH

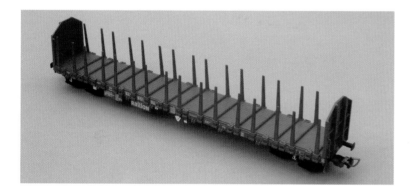

A DB Roos stake wagon by Piko straight out of the box. In reality, a wagon would only look this clean on its first day in service. This model needs weathering to look more realistic.

Just by painting the floor dark grey and weathering the wagon it looks a lot better. The writing and logos were slightly distressed with a glass-fibre brush to tone down the appearance of the wagon. Real wagons that regularly carry logs are rarely in pristine condition and get quite 'bashed around' by the constant movement of logs in and out of the wagon.

MODELLING A TIMBER-LOADING SIDING

Timber sidings are easy to reproduce in miniature and do not require too much space. The basic elements are a rail siding (or two) with road access, plus an area of level ground adjacent to the siding(s) for the storage of logs and trans-shipment on to the rail wagons or a side-loading platform. Timber can be loaded on to the rail wagons either from ground level or from a raised platform, or directly from a lorry where it has a body-mounted crane.

The area around a real timber siding is usually covered with bits of timber and bark that have fallen off the tree trunks whilst the loading process was taking place. The debris can be made from ground-up bits of twig and real earth fixed to the baseboard using diluted PVA adhesive applied through a plastic syringe or eye dropper.

Piles of logs alongside the track waiting to be loaded on to rail wagons can be made from twigs collected from your garden. Other alternatives could be piles of logs from Ten Commandments, Harburn Hobbies and others, though in my experience nothing looks more realistic than twigs and real wood.

Moving real logs around at a saw mill at Niedersill in Austria on the Pinzgau narrow-gauge line on 8 October 2013.

The area around a real timber siding is usually covered in bits of timber and bark that have fallen off the tree trunks whilst the loading process was taking place.

ABOVE LEFT: Here is the timber-loading siding before the addition of log debris and weeds. The track has been weathered using a brown acrylic aerosol.

ABOVE RIGHT: I sprinkled on finely chopped real bark to represent leftover bits of bark that are seen on real timber-loading sidings. Other options are 'over the counter' products from Treemendus and WW Scenics.

ABOVE LEFT: **The log and tree bark debris can be made from ground-up bits of twig and real earth fixed to the baseboard using diluted PVA adhesive applied through a plastic syringe or an eye dropper.**

ABOVE RIGHT: **Bark and log debris lies adjacent to the timber siding as a worker wearing a hard hat looks on. The grass tuft represents a big weed that has taken hold.**

BELOW: **Weathered Roco SBB Cargo Class 203 diesel locomotive with an Eaos wagon by Liliput that has been loaded with logs (twigs from the garden).**

MODELLING TIMBER LOADS FOR WAGONS

Generally logs are not allowed to protrude above the stakes on wagons by more than half the log's diameter without being secured. Logs with a diameter of more than 70cm have to be secured individually. When loading beech, oak or timber from wet storage wagons, the maximum load weight can be easily exceeded by the sheer weight of the water inside the logs.

To model a load of logs, collect a selection of twigs from your garden, local park or on a woodland walk. Use pieces measuring up to 5mm across if you are working in HO scale; it is best to work with logs that are fully dried before cutting them. If the twigs are damp, leave them in a warm room or the airing cupboard to dry before cutting them. When selecting the twigs that you want to use as wagonloads, it is best only to use those that are nearly straight and roughly similar in diameter on the same wagon.

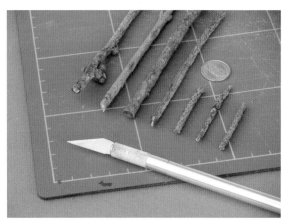

ABOVE LEFT: **Comparing a bundle of plastic logs with real twigs. The plastic logs would benefit from some judicious painting and weathering but would they ever look as good as real twigs? Probably not.**

ABOVE RIGHT: **Different sizes of twigs can be collected. Only collect those twigs that are straight. The twigs can be trimmed over a self sealing cutting board.**

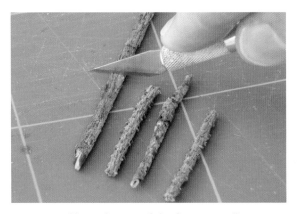

ABOVE LEFT: **Use a sharp craft knife or a small saw to cut the twigs so as to leave the end with a 'clean' cut so that it will look its most realistic.**

ABOVE RIGHT: **A bundle of cut twigs from my garden held together with PVA adhesive. These would be ideal as a load on a stake wagon.**

ABOVE LEFT: This load of logs was made using a piece of polystyrene foam as the central core. In this way less twigs will be needed though the end will need to be disguised in some way such as using it in wagons that have full end sections.

ABOVE RIGHT: A pile of cut logs in weed-strewn sidings. The static grass was planted using a Noch Gras-master.

A woodcutter by Noch, who may have rather a long job ahead of him judging by the size of the log he has chosen to cut.

Cleanly cut off any side shoots as near to the main stalk as possible using a sharp craft knife and a cutting board. Cut the lengths with a new blade rather than leaving a ragged edge and where the twigs are of larger size it may be best to use a small saw to cut through them rather than a craft knife. Even twigs that are slightly bent can be used as loads by choosing the straightest parts of the twig, then cutting out those parts to use. If there are any loose pieces of bark left over, keep these so that you can crush them between your fingers to represent the debris around the sidings.

Alternatively, fix twigs around a piece of polystyrene or hard foam. The advantage of this is that you do not have to use so many twigs for each load and the hard foam centre will be light in weight.

In real life, as the accompanying pictures show, timber-carrying wagons are always pretty dirty and 'bashed around', because logs have been loaded on and off them frequently. To make the model wagons look more realistic, some weathering is essential. In addition, the loads need some visible securing to make them look complete. It takes about an hour to weather a wagon, add the load and the strapping. This time does not include the drying times for the various adhesives, paint and dyes. Cut thin strips of cardboard using a steel ruler and a sharp craft knife to represent the strapping on the wagons. These can be dark red, blue, black or grey.

Ready-made log loads for timber-carrying wagons are made by a number of other companies including Duha and Lädegutter Bauer.

An unloaded wagon with leftover bark and bits of tree on the wagon floor is an eye-catching feature, rather than having all the wagons loaded with timber.

The Roco model of an Ealos wagon as it comes straight out of the box. The supplied load of timber sits too low in the wagon, there is a pack of detailing parts to be fitted and it all looks just too clean.

ABOVE LEFT: *The Roco Ealos wagon following the addition of some of the red detailing parts plus the timber load, which has been raised about 4mm by adding cardboard underneath the supplied Roco load.*

ABOVE RIGHT: *Detail picture of an Ealos wagon at Worgl, Austria, on 7 October 2013, showing a patch of new paint.*

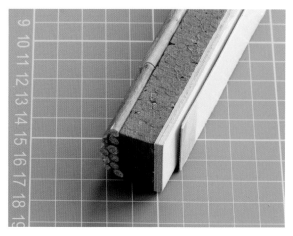

ABOVE LEFT: *I used pieces of Tamiya masking tape to create the effect of new patches of paint on the side of the wagon. The wagon would then be sprayed with an aerosol of acrylic paint.*

ABOVE RIGHT: *To build up the level of the logs in the wagon, I added several pieces of thick cardboard to the base of the supplied load. The cardboard was attached with PVA adhesive.*

After weathering the wagon, the strap connections are toned down and the patches of new paint stand out from the remainder of the dirty and tired wagon.

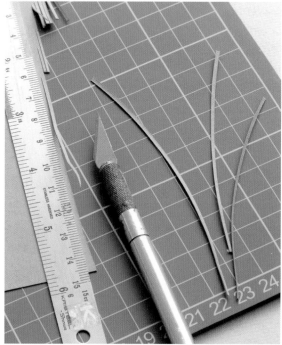

ABOVE: *Here are the thin strips of cardboard being cut out to represent securing straps on the wagon. It is definitely worth using a new blade when doing this to ensure that the cuts are clean, with no ragged edges.*

LEFT: *To make thin strips representing the straps holding the load of logs, I carefully cut 1mm strips of thin cardboard with a sharp craft knife and steel ruler over a self-sealing cutting board. I then used small drops of UHU Holz Leim quick-drying adhesive to fix the straps to the wagon.*

ABOVE: *The straps were held in place with a little adhesive at the top and bottom of each side of the wagon. To colour the straps, I used black wash with a small paintbrush. The wagon is still to be weathered, which will hide the small glossy patches of dried adhesive.*

RIGHT: *The excess length of the strap was cut off with a sharp craft knife once the end had been secured with the dried adhesive.*

The straps in position on a weathered Ealos wagon. Looking at this wagon again, I think that more straps should have been added.

LEFT: The finished Roco DB Ealos wagon – compare this to the wagon depicted in the first picture of this sequence. The detail parts have been fitted, the wagon has been weathered, patches of fresh paint are on the sides, the load of logs has been raised and securing tapes have been added.

BELOW: ÖBB 2043 019 locomotive by Roco awaits a green light before moving off with its load of logs.

The following tools and materials will be needed:

- selection of small paintbrushes for the paint and dyes
- acrylic paints
- weathering dyes
- black insulation tape or thin cardboard for the strapping
- sharp craft knife and steel ruler for cutting the strapping into thin lengths
- self-sealing cutting mat
- PVA adhesive to glue down the load
- matt varnish as a last step of weathering
- Treemendus or WW Scenics forest floor scatter material for wagons without loads.

ÖBB 2043 019 shunting loaded Eanos wagons in the yard.

Sawn logs are stacked up alongside the 760mm track at on Pinzgau Bahn at Niedersill in Austria.

THE FORESTRY CYCLE

The forestry cycle usually follows a regular pattern:

- Preparation of the ground for the tree seedlings. Where the ground is level (such as on lower slopes or the valley floors), a tractor and plough may be used to turn the ground. The planting of the seedlings is mainly done by hand.
- Thinning of the forest because more trees are initially planted in the ground than will be needed. The poorer-quality trees will be removed over the growing life of the trees.
- Felling of the trees, which take between 40 and 150 years of growth to reach a maturity, becoming suitable for being harvested.
- Removal of the felled trees, with road vehicles and mechanical grabbers taking the felled logs from the forest along dirt tracks to the main roads, then onwards to trans-shipment points, or to the railway sidings.

The Volvo logger by Atlas loads the last two logs into the DB Ealos wagon.

MOVING TIMBER AND ITS PRODUCTS BY RAIL

- Logs are moved from railheads near the forests to sawmills and pulp mills.
- Logs and cut timber are moved to timber merchants and to chalet builders in Alpine countries.
- Paper from pulp mills is moved to distribution centres and to newspaper printers.
- Wooden fencing is moved from factories to distribution centres. MDF, particleboard, chipboard and others are moved from board producers to distribution centres.

Lowering the timber on to a DB HO-scale stake wagon.

Timber loading using a Volvo logging vehicle by Atlas with a grab that can be opened and closed and raised. The land adjacent to the siding was covered in PVA adhesive then real sand sprinkled on to the wet adhesive to and left to dry. The figures are by Preiser.

continued overleaf

MOVING TIMBER AND ITS PRODUCTS BY RAIL *continued*

Timber loading using a couple of weed-strewn sidings. The static grass was planted using a Noch Gras-master and the earth surrounding the sidings is fine real earth by Treemendus Models. The figures are by Preiser, the hut is a plastic kit by Atlas and the Volvo logging vehicle is by Atlas. The locomotive and wagon are by Fleischmann.

Detail picture showing the load of real twigs in position on the Sps wagon by Piko with bogies that were weathered using Tamiya chalks.

CHAPTER FOURTEEN

MODELLING EUROPE'S HIGH-SPEED TRAINS

The expanding high-speed rail network opens up Europe.

There is now an excellent European network of high-speed lines to compete with competition from air and road. Various high-speed lines are in service, some are under construction and many still are at the drawing-board stage. Countries, including Belgium, France, Germany, Italy, Spain and Switzerland, already have high-speed lines. Britain has a high-speed connection with the European high-speed network, with line HS1 from London St Pancras International to the Channel Tunnel. At the time of writing, there is much controversy surrounding the building of the second high-speed line in the UK known as HS2.

Europe's high-speed trains include the German ICE, France's TGV, Sweden's X2000, various Italian Pendolinos, Italy's privately owned Italo sets, Spain's AVE, Switzerland's ICN, the pan-European Thalys sets and the tri-country Eurostar trains. The trains are a mixed bag – some of these high-speed trains are tilting trains and others have double-deck carriages. Whilst most of these trains are operated by the national rail operators, in Italy the privately owned Italo company uses the latest high-speed AGV train sets from Alstom. New Eurostar train sets are due in 2015 and these are expected to link London directly with Switzerland and the Netherlands, in addition to France and Belgium.

The definition of high speed is not clear: there are dedicated high-speed lines on which trains travel at up to 300km/h and above, then there are 'classic' tracks that are used by tilting trains that might also be classified as high speed. And what is high speed in one country might not be considered to meet that criterion in another country. For example, in the UK the well-known HST travels at up to 200km/h, but the West Coast Pendolinos are designed for 225km/h. And in some European countries 160km/h is considered to be high speed.

INTEGRATING EUROPE'S HIGH-SPEED NETWORK

Ideally, Europe's railways should have a greater degree of uniformity, which would allow trains to cross borders without the need to change motive power at the borders. However, various major obstacles have to be addressed before an integrated European rail network is fully established, including the different power supplies of the countries and indeed the multiple different power voltages within some countries, various signalling methods, varying standards of rolling-stock technology and the various track gauges. These obstacles are slowly being overcome by building rolling stock with several voltage capabilities (for example, Eurostar, Thalys and locomotives such as Traxx), the installation of various signalling equipment within the motive power and new rolling stock and locomotives being built to more common European standards.

The first high-speed European line was the French Ligne à Grand Vitesse Sud-Est that opened in 1981. This was followed by other French high-speed lines, including Atlantique, Rhône Alps, Nord Europe, Jonction and the Mediterranean. These dedicated new lines use TGV trains, which give substantial journey time reductions compared with classic lines with locomotive-hauled stock.

In Germany, various Neubaustrecke (new build lines) have opened since 1991. These included stretches between Hanover and Berlin; Mannheim and Stuttgart; Cologne and Frankfurt and more.

The 180km Cologne to Frankfurt Neubaustrecke opened in 2002, cutting the Cologne to Frankfurt rail journey time in half.

In 1991, the high-speed line between Madrid and Seville opened in Spain, which was followed by other lines to Malaga, Valencia and Barcelona, with more being under construction. Whilst Italy now has high-speed lines between Turin, Milan, Rome and Naples, its main contribution to rapid rail travel has been the development of tilting trains for the domestic and worldwide market. The 88km Belgian high-speed line (Belge LGV) reduced the Eurostar journey between Brussels and London by fifteen minutes.

Whilst some countries opt for new high-speed lines, others have less scope to build them – for example, Switzerland's landscape means that it has little scope for building new long high-speed lines. It has tackled this problem by building some new lines, such as the double-track line between Mattstetten and Rothrist for 200km/h passenger train running that opened on 12 December 2004. In addition, the Lötschberg AlpTransit Tunnel opened in 2007 and in 2016 the AlpTransit Gotthard Tunnels will open to reduce journey times across Switzerland.

AVE

AVE (Alta Velocidad Española) is the name given to the Spanish high-speed rail network. Owned by the Spanish National Railways, Renfe, the AVE lines are still being expanded. The high-speed line between Madrid and Seville uses twenty AVE train sets, which were built in France using some Spanish components derived directly from the French TGV Atlantique, with a top speed of 300km/h. Their noses are more rounded that the TGV and there are other detail changes, with each set carrying 313 passengers.

The Altaria is a high-speed long-distance train that connects the Spanish capital Madrid to the southern cities of Algeciras, Granada, Cartagena and Murcia. Altaria trains are uniquely designed, with gauge-changing technology enabling them to travel on both standard and high-speed rails, reaching speeds of up to 200 km/h.

MODELS

In HO scale, Electrotren produces models of Alaris, AVE, Euromed and Talgo. Mehano produces various AVE sets and for N scale Arnold produces models of AVE and Talgo trains.

EUROSTAR

Eurostar, or TransManche Super Trains (TMST), link London with Paris and Brussels. Each train cost £24 million and they are classified as BR Class 373, with a permitted maximum speed of 300km/h. These are technically the most complex units to operate in the UK, being based on the successful French TGV Atlantique design, with an output of 16,408hp (12,240Kw). New Eurostar sets based on the DB Velaro train set will be introduced into service in late 2015.

MODELS

In HO scale, Jouef produces a Eurostar set and Hornby produces a model in OO scale in the old and new livery. Kato produces a model of Eurostar in N scale.

ICE

Germany's Inter-City Express (ICE) trains first entered service in June 1991 and over 250 units of various types provide services within Germany and onwards to various countries, including Austria, Belgium, Denmark, France, the Netherlands and Switzerland. ICE represents Deutsche Bahn's high-speed train, running at up to 280km/h (ICE1 and ICE2), or 300km/h (ICE3) on dedicated high-speed lines and up to 209km/h over upgraded conventional lines. The ICE is one of Europe's most comfortable, civilized and impressive high-speed trains, with a very high-spec interior. There are two tilting versions, the electric ICE-T and diesel ICE-TD.

MODELS

In HO scale, Fleischmann, Märklin, Roco and Trix produce various models of the ICE. In N scale, Minitrix and Tillig retail models.

Eurostar, or TransManche Super Trains, link London with Paris and Brussels. Set 3208 was seen at London St Pancras International station on 19 October 2010.

Germany's ICE trains first entered service in June 1991. Over 250 units of various types provide services to and from Germany to Austria, Belgium, Denmark, France, Netherlands and Switzerland. This ICE set stands at London St Pancras International station on 19 October 2010, where DB announced its plans to operate ICE trains to and from the UK.

ICN

SBB/CFF/FFS, as the operator of Switzerland's rail network, introduced a 44-strong fleet of tilting trains, enabling many services to be increased in frequency to half-hourly because of infrastructure improvements and the introduction of these trains. The ICN sets were supplied by a consortium of major manufacturers, comprising Alstom, Adtranz (now Bombardier), Fiat-SIG and Schindler Waggon. The 200km/h trains are known as Inter-City ICN (Intercity-Neigezug), or InterCity tilting train, and these RABDe 500 sets often run with two complete trains, each with seven carriages, both including a dining car (which forms part of second class).

MODELS

In HO scale, Roco makes a model of the train set.

PENDOLINO

Pendolino (Italian for tilting) sets operate in a number of countries, including China, the Czech Republic, Italy, Finland, Poland, Portugal, Russia, Slovenia, Slovakia, Spain, Switzerland and the UK (Virgin Pendolinos).

A tilting SBB ICN set between Lausanne and Geneva on 10 February 2015.

Over 500 trains equipped with Pendolino technology have been sold to date, operating in thirteen countries and crossing seven borders. Thanks to the Tiltronix anticipatory tilting technology, Pendolinos can travel more rapidly through curves on conventional lines (35 per cent faster than a classic train) and up to 250km/h on high-speed lines, while guaranteeing good passenger comfort inside the train, even on the most winding sections of track. Alstom now produces these trains.

MODELS

In HO scale, Rivarossi produces models of various Pendolino sets, including the ETR 450. In the Lima Expert range the SBB ETR 610 is produced and ACME has announced a model of the ETR 250 and ETR 610 sets.

ABOVE: **Over 500 trains equipped with Pendolino technology have been sold to date, operating in thirteen countries and crossing seven borders. Here, one of the SBB ETR 610 sets stands at Milano Central on 25 October 2009 in the early SBB livery.**

RIGHT: **The ceiling-mounted information screen inside an SBB ETR 610 Pendolino set from Geneva to Milan on EC 39 on 10 February 2015. As the journey progressed, the map was updated and information of connecting services supplied.**

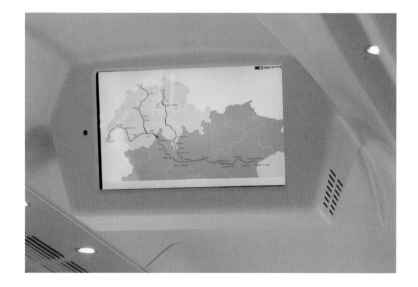

RAILJET

Austria's flagship trains are the Railjet (RJ) high-speed trains that operate between Austria, Germany, Hungary and Switzerland. Railjet trains are modern locomotive-hauled trains reaching speeds of up to 230km/h. Railjet operates from Vienna to Salzburg and on to Innsbruck, Bregenz and Zürich, as well as from Vienna to Graz, Klagenfurt and Villach, or from Munich to Vienna and on to Budapest. Other destinations include Stuttgart, Mannheim, Frankfurt, Brno and Prague.

MODELS

In HO scale, Jägerndorfer and Roco produce models of the Railjet sets in various versions. Hobbytrain produces sets in N scale and Fleischmann makes the locomotives.

TGV

French Railways' TGV (Train à Grande Vitesse) trains were the first European high-speed trains. France's first high-speed line ran between Paris and Lyon and was opened in stages between 1981 and 1983 and during the first twenty-five years of operation TGV trains carried more than 1.2 billion passengers. The current TGV domestic networks are the TGV Atlantique, operating between Paris, Tours, Le Mans and other destinations in west and south-west France; Sud-Est and Rhône Alps routes linking Paris with Lyon, Valence and other destinations in south and east France. This route has been extended southwards by the LGV Mediterranean line to Marseille and Nimes; Nord Europe route northwards from Paris to Lille, Calais, the Channel Tunnel, Brussels and Amsterdam; and Est to

Railjet high-speed trains operate between Austria, Germany, Hungary and Switzerland at speeds up to 230km/h. On 11 May 2011, a Railjet set stands at Salzburg main station.

Strasbourg. The TGV networks extend beyond the French borders, with the Atlantique route continuing into Spain and the Sud-Est route to Switzerland and Italy.

The original SNCF TGV livery was mainly orange, but it has now become standardized in blue, grey and silver. Special advertising liveries have been carried on a few TGV and Eurostar sets. The train sets of a cut-price TGV service named Ouigo carry a vivid blue livery.

A Swiss/Franco consortium known as TGV Lyria currently manages TGV units operating between Paris, Basle, Bern, Geneva, Interlaken, Lausanne, Neuchâtel and Zürich. Some of these routes are extended during the skiing season.

TGV train sets comprise a power car at each end and various numbers of intermediate trailer carriages.

The Sud-Est and Nord Europe sets have eight trailers. There are ten in the Atlantique sets and eighteen on the Eurostar. The third-generation TGV sets are TGV Duplex double-deck sets, which were initially introduced on the Paris to Lyon services. These have a smoother aerodynamic shape and carry a grey/blue livery. With its double-deck design, a TGV Duplex can carry 40 per cent more passengers than the conventional train.

MODELS

In HO scale, Jouef and Mehano produce a selection of TGV models, including single- and double-deck sets, La Poste and Ouigo versions. Märklin produces a TGV Lyria set in HO scale. In N scale, Kato makes a number of versions, including Duplex double-deck stock and TGV Lyria.

French Railways' TGV trains were the first European high-speed trains. During the first twenty-five years of operation, TGV trains have carried more than 1.2 billion passengers. Depicted at Nice station is a TGV Duplex set.

A single-deck TGV speeds through La Plaine on a service from Geneva to Paris. The village of La Plaine stands at the border of France and Switzerland.

THALYS

Thalys train sets (based on TGVs) are used on the Paris, Brussels, Cologne and Amsterdam (PBKA) services. On 8 October 2013, Thalys carried its one-millionth passenger, with the Thalys fleet currently comprising of seventeen trains equipped with 4V systems and seven signalling systems to operate over the entire Thalys network, plus nine Thalys PBA (Paris–Brussels–Amsterdam) trains equipped with 3V systems. The Thalys livery is maroon and grey.

MODELS

In HO scale, Mehano produces Thalys train sets, with an N scale set from Kato.

MODEL OVERVIEW

All of these models are ideal for the Epoch V/VI period and the prototypes are all in daily operation today. Most of the high-speed train sets are sold as a four-car pack (two driving ends and two intermediate carriages), with some packs of three intermediate carriages being sold separately.

WHERE CAN I SEE THESE TRAINS?

Lille is a good place to start. By arriving on a Euro-star from the UK, onward destinations can be reached using Thalys, TGV Atlantique, TGV Lyria and TGV

Whilst not strictly a high-speed train set, the Trans Europ Express used to be one of Europe's most prestigious trains. This HO-scale model is by Rivarossi.

Duplex to places such as Amsterdam, Lyon, Bordeaux, the French Riviera, Cologne, Bern and Geneva. Over 100 million people live within a two-hour rail journey of Lille Europe station, which is just 90 minutes from London St Pancras International station using Eurostar services. Most travellers agree that European high-speed trains are very comfortable. To watch the countryside going past at speeds of up to 300km/h is a most enjoyable way to travel. It beats the queues at airports!

As mentioned above, there are various locations (for example, Lille) where several different types of high-speed trains can be seen working side by side. At other locations they can be seen working alongside 'classic' loco-hauled rolling stock and in addition all the units are, for some parts of their journeys, on 'normal' non-high-speed track (even if that is just in the run-up to the station platforms). The modelling potential of thus running a French TGV on an adjacent track to a Swiss, Italian or Spanish locomotive is there. These sets can be used much more flexibly

than could be first imagined, because they are not limited to working on high-speed tracks.

EURO-MODELLING INTERLUDE – INSPIRATION FROM THE ONTRAXS SHOW

Each March a model railway show is held at the Utrecht Spoorwegmuseum (Dutch Railway Museum), with layouts coming from various parts of Europe. For more information about past and future shows go to www.ontraxs.com and www.teammitropa.nl.

One of the layouts that caught visitors' attention in 2011 was the HO-scale layout built by Michael Kirsch on top of IKEA shelving units. It took just four months to build and includes a quayside, factories, a small passing station and a farm. The layout measured 3.75 × 0.4m. To the right-hand side looking at the layout was a 0.80m storage yard. The track used was Tillig Elite and many of the buildings were made from kits by Auhagen.

The Italo logo. This privately owned company operates high-speed rail services between Torino, Milano, Roma and other cities in Italy.

Italo high-speed set made by Alstom stands at Torino on 10 February 2015.

ABOVE: *At the Ontraxs 2011 model railway exhibition in Utrecht, the Netherlands, this layout was built on IKEA bookshelves. Looking along the entire 3.75m scenic section of the layout, there is a factory, a small passing station, a quayside and a farm.*

RIGHT: *The support for the layout is a series of bookshelves by IKEA. These good value for money items of furniture evidentially offer a quick and easy self-assembly way of providing support for small layouts. The layout was built by Michael Kirsch.*

ABOVE: *Though the width of the baseboard is only 40cm, it still provides room for a good level of detail and facilities.*

LEFT: *Many of the industrial buildings on this layout were made from Auhagen modular parts that are available in the UK from Golden Valley Hobbies.*

CHAPTER FIFTEEN

A CASE STUDY – MODELLING AUSTRIA'S RAILWAYS

How to go about making a first layout based on Austria.

Austria is located in Central Europe, bordering with the Czech Republic, Germany, Hungary, Italy, Liechtenstein, Slovakia, Slovenia and Switzerland. The landlocked country is around 84,000sq km, being roughly 560km from east to west and 280km from north to south. Austria's population is over 8 million, with more than 1.76 million of that number in its capital, Vienna. The next largest cities are Graz, Innsbruck, Linz and Salzburg.

Austria features mountainous regions, hill country and plains, with much of the country being forested. There are approximately 3,200 cable cars, chair lifts and ski lifts and many of these reach altitudes of up to 3,000m and hence the country is popular with tourists in both summer and winter. Austria's highest mountain is 3,797m and the country's main river is the famous Danube, with a length of about 350km within the national borders. The Danube has excellent cycle tracks for tourists.

Austrian ÖBB Class 1044 locomotive by Roco pulls a Swiss-based Eaos wagon filled with cut logs on the author's AlpMitholz layout.

WHY MODEL AUSTRIAN RAILWAYS?

One reason that immediately springs to mind is the magnificent scenery, but the railway aspects of the country enhance that. Today, there is an extensive standard-gauge network with both electrified and diesel operated lines, plus the extensive movement of freight, including wagonload trains. There are various narrow-gauge networks that link with the standard-gauge network and in some cases standard-gauge wagons run on special wagons on the narrow-gauge lines to delivery points.

There are various tourist mountain lines with steam haulage and over the course of each year there are classic diesel, electric and steam-hauled excursions operated on main and secondary lines.

THE RAILWAYS OF AUSTRIA TODAY

The Austrian Federal Railway (Österreichische Bundesbahnen – ÖBB) network links all Austria's major cities, with good connections to neighbouring European countries and cities. The country's rail network has around 4,900km of standard-gauge track, with 400km of 760mm-gauge track, the remaining 15km being metre gauge. Over 80 per cent of the ÖBB network is electrified and in addition to the ÖBB, twelve independent companies operate over 620km of track using a variety of gauges. Sadly, some of the lesser used lines, including much of the narrow-gauge network, have, or are being, cut back in 'Beeching-style' closure plans.

The main Austrian passenger routes are: the Westbahn linking Vienna with Linz and Salzburg; the Semmering route from Vienna to Graz; the Tauern Tunnel line between Salzburg and Villach; the Arlberg line through Innsbruck and the Tirol; and the Brenner line from Innsbruck to Italy.

The ÖBB operates a wide range of passenger services including the following:

- Railjet are the newest trains in Austria at the time of writing, with three classes of accommodation: Premium Class, First Class and Economy Class. These locomotive-hauled trains feature a Taurus locomotive, a driving trailer and intermediate carriages. The Railjet network centres on Vienna to Budapest, to Graz, to Munich and to Zürich via Salzburg and Innsbruck.
- EuroCity (EC) trains are prestige services operating between major European cities.

Early stages of an Austrian layout using both standard-gauge HO track and narrow-gauge HOe track. The HO ÖBB Class 5022 unit is by Piko, with the narrow-gauge stock by Liliput.

There are daily EuroCity services linking Austria with Rome, Budapest, Prague, Warsaw, Berlin, Munich, Zürich, Basle, Paris, Bucharest and others. Germany's Inter-City Express (ICE Class 411) trains are used on some of the EuroCity services linking Austria with Germany.

- Inter-City (IC) trains along with the EC services carry names. The longest internal IC service operates between Vienna and Bregenz via Salzburg and Innsbruck. Some services are designated ÖBB EC and ÖBB IC to highlight their exclusivity.
- Regional Express, or Regionalzüge, services are usually worked with City Sprinter carriages with a driving-end EMU, or DMUs operating regular interval push–pull (mainly) second-class trains between the main towns. Most carriages are usually grey and red and feature the name of the route, for example Salzburg Linie and Tirol Takt. The City Sprinter trains are usually formed of two carriages upwards and are loco-hauled, either using a diesel or electric locomotive. Both single- and double-deck carriages are used and many of the single-deck City Sprinter carriages are refurbished older carriages.
- Express trains (D) are ordinary express trains sometimes known as Schnellzug.

- Local stopping trains use older stock but are being replaced by Talent EMUs and Desiro DMUs.

Today, the national rail operator has competition in the form of Westbahn, which operates regular passenger services between Vienna and Salzburg. Liliput makes an HO-scale model of the Stadler KISS Westbahn trains that are used on this route (for more information go to www.westbahn.at).

There are frequent national and international freight services and wagonload traffic is still popular in Austria, together with block trains and 'rolling road' HGV-carrying trains.

Until recently, the most common locomotives were the Bo-Bo Classes 1042, some of which date from 1963, and 1044, introduced in 1974. Push–pull versions of the 1042 locomotives are designated 1142. A new general-purpose locomotive was introduced in 1999, known as Taurus, forming Classes 1016, 1116 and 1216. On moving off, these locomotives emit the musical sound of 'do-re-mi'! Some of the locomotive classes are dual-voltage for cross-border working to Italy, Hungary and Slovakia.

The diesel fleet includes mixed traffic locomotives, shunting locomotives and a variety of multiple units, including Desiro two-car DMUs (Class 5022) and single-car DMUs classified as Class 5047.

Classic and modern DMUs at Rotenegg, north of Linz. Nearest the camera are two Class 5047 single-car units, with a two-car Siemens Desiro Class 5022 about to depart back to Linz Urfahr on 10 May 2011.

LEFT: Cycling is very popular in Austria, especially along the River Danube. Wagons carry bikes on some designated passenger trains.

BELOW: Private enterprise Westbahn operates trains between Vienna and Salzburg. Here, one of its units built by Stadler stands at the colourful rebuilt station at Salzburg on 30 April 2012. HO-scale models of these KISS EMUs introduced by Westbahn are available from Liliput. The carriages are double-deck and are sold as a four-car set, plus an add-on pack of two additional centre carriages featuring on/off LED interior lighting.

BELOW: Modern Talent ÖBB Class 4024 EMU on 1 May 2012. Models of these EMUs are available from Brawa in HO scale.

The modern general-purpose locomotives introduced from 1999 have been known as Taurus of Classes 1016, 1116 and 1216. On moving off, these locomotives emit the musical sound of 'do-re-mi'! Some other locomotive Classes (1014, 1114 and 1822) are dual-voltage for cross-border working to Italy, Hungary and Slovakia. Models of these locomotives are available in N, TT, HO and O scales. Locomotive 1116 213 was pictured on 2 April 2009 at Villach station.

Railjet locomotive 1116 219 stands at Salzburg station on 11 May 2011.

ÖBB diesel Tractor at Wernstein station on 10 May 2011.

Single-car DMU Class 5047 099 in new ÖBB livery stands at Aigen Schlägl station at the end of the line from Linz.

Salzburger Lokalbahn Taurus 91 stands at Salzburg Hbf on 2 April 2009.

ÖBB shunting locomotive Class 2068 036 at Villach station on 2 April 2009. Models of these locomotives are available in HO scale from Klein Modellbahn.

ÖBB Class 2016 at Brenner station on 13 July 2012 on track-maintenance trains whilst the Brenner Pass line was being rebuilt.

NARROW-GAUGE RAILWAYS

Various narrow-gauge lines were built in Austria, including 760mm gauge and metre gauge. Two tram networks were built with the gauge of 900mm.

The 760mm-gauge electrified Mariazellerbahn travels along the Pielach Valley in the Mostviertel region, past the Ötscher mountain and into the Mariazell region. It opened in 1906 and has a length of 84km, with a difference in altitude of 619m. Its longest tunnel is 2.369km and the longest viaduct is 113m long.

Also in 760mm gauge, the Pinzgauer Lokalbahn (Pinzgauer local railway) runs through the heart of the Pinzgau region. It opened in 1898 and the line leads through the valley from the lakeside resort of Zell am See to the mountainous village of Krimml, which is famous for its waterfalls. The line follows the River Salzach and after the destructive floods of 2005 the line was rebuilt between Mittersill and Krimml and since reopening in late 2010 the 53km-long route has been served by historic steam and diesel locomotives. In 2014, there was more damage done to the line by floods and again part of the line had to be rebuilt.

The Zillertalbahn Railway (760mm), operating along the Zillertal Valley, was founded in 1899 and has a cross-platform connection with the ÖBB main line at Jenbach. The 32km route is operated using diesel and steam traction, carrying around 2 million passengers each year.

TRAMS

There are extensive tram networks in Graz, Innsbruck, Salzburg and Vienna. For example, there are six tram lines in Graz and these constitute the backbone of public transport.

VIENNA MAIN STATION

After five years of construction, the new Vienna Main Station opened on 14 December 2014 and trains

Krimml station on 8 October 2013. It is the terminus of the Pinzgauer Lokalbahn line from Zell am See. Steam and diesel services operate on this beautiful line.

from all directions now arrive in Austria's capital at this modern through station with connections to many European cities. Vienna has strengthened its position at the railway centre of Europe, as all long-distance trains to/from the south (Italy, Slovenia, Graz and Villach), east (Budapest) and north (Brno, Prague, Warsaw) now stop at Vienna Main Station. Also from that date, all overnight and motorail trains to/from Vienna originate and terminate at Vienna Main Station, together with direct services to Germany and Switzerland.

From December 2015, all ÖBB long-distance services to/from Vienna will use the new main station with its good links to the public transport system, underground and suburban train lines. In addition, Vienna International Airport will be better connected to the long-distance rail network with Railjet and Inter-City trains on the Westbahn line travelling directly to

the airport. Over 1,000 trains and around 145,000 passengers will use the new station daily.

SEMMERINGBAHN

Austria's Semmeringbahn with a length of 41.7km was the first railway to cross the Alps and celebrated its 150th anniversary in 2004. Whilst the distance on the ground from Gloggnitz (in Lower Austria/Niederösterreich) and Mürzzuschlag (in Styria/Steiermark) is only 21km, the sinuous route taken by the railway doubles the distance of the track. The northern ramp from Gloggnitz to Semmering is 28.4km long, with the southern ramp from Mürzzuschlag to Semmering being 13.3km in length. The maximum gradient on the northern ramp is 1:40, with the maximum gradient on the southern ramp being 1:45, and the sharpest radius on the line is 190m. The difference in altitude over the line is 459m above sea level, between Glog-gnitz at 439m above sea level and the peak of the line at 898m in the Semmering Tunnel. There are sixteen viaducts on the line, with an overall length of 1,607m. The highest viaduct crosses the Kalte Rinne near Bre-itenstein at 46m high and in addition there are fifteen tunnels on the line, with an overall length of 4,526m.

Compared to other international railway lines, which have been extensively updated and modern-ized since the original building, most of the Semmer-ingbahn is in its original state. Later changes include the addition of a second peak tunnel in 1952 and the electrification of the line in the 1950s, but most of the viaducts, the station buildings, tunnel portals and lines-man houses have simply been updated rather than re-built. The Semmeringbahn has been protected under the Austrian Law of Protection of Monuments since 1923 and the Austrian Federal Office of Monuments reconfirmed this status in March 1997. UNESCO was so impressed with the blend of the railway into the landscape that it added the Semmeringbahn to its World Heritage list in December 1998 alongside the statue of Liberty and Stonehenge. The notable railway construction in difficult terrain, the good condition of the buildings and also the visual image of the railway line within the landscape contributed to their decision.

MODELLING AUSTRIAN RAILWAYS

Many of the secondary routes in Austria are single track, so with a simple track plan an ideal exhibi-tion layout could be built. Around 20 per cent of the standard-gauge lines in Austria are not electrified, so if you prefer diesel power there is no need to erect a catenary system. That said, Hobbex and Sommerfeldt manufacture ÖBB-style catenary with colour light signals being available from Alphamodell, Schneider and Viessmann.

Chalets and station buildings can be modelled us-ing plastic and laser-cut kits available from a number of manufacturers, including Auhagen, Busch, Faller, Kibri and Noch. Brekina, Busch, Kibri and others pro-duce models of farm vehicles to make an agricultural scene in country areas. Figures are available from Merten, Noch and Preiser. Cars and road vehicles are made by Busch, Herpa, Kibri, Reitze, VK Modelle, Wiking and others.

Austrian layouts require a lot of trees and under-growth. Please see Chapter 7 on the European land-scape for information about manufacturers. Busch, Kibri, Jowi, MZZ and Vollmer produce backscenes that incorporate locations resembling the rolling hills and mountains of Austria.

Roco ÖBB 2043 loco with a couple of Inter-City (ÖBB IC) carriages.

With regular motive power being a mixture of diesel and electric, this adds an extra dimension not normally found at locations with catenary (where usually electric motive power prevails to the exclusion of diesel). In HO scale, for example, all the main locomotive types are readily available from Brawa, Fleischmann, Jägerndorfer, Kleinbahn, Piko, Rivarossi, Roco, TI-HO and more. Ferro Train, Halling, Hapo, Liliput, MiniTrains, Roco, Stangl and others produce models of the narrow-gauge rolling stock in HO scale.

ABOVE: *Model of ÖBB 2068 055 by Klein Modellbahn. This is one of my best-running locomotives and can be controlled to move very slowly.*

LEFT: *Just some of the superb small details on a Roco ÖBB Class 2016 Hercules loco in HO scale.*

ABOVE: *Out in the country a Roco ÖBB 1044 290 locomotive pulls a mixed goods train towards Linz.*

RIGHT: *Classic ÖBB traction in the form of locomotive Class 1010 014 by Roco on the author's layout.*

Rail Cargo Austria logo on a nearly new Habbins bogie wagon.

The Rail Cargo Austria logo on a Roco model of the Habbins bogie wagon.

Sliding-door goods wagon at Jenbach on the Zillertalbahn (ZB) narrow-gauge line carrying the Liliput livery of the company that produces many of the ZB models in HOe scale, 9 October 2013.

The buffet wagon of the Zillertalbahn at Jenbach, Austria, on 9 October 2013.

*RIGHT: **The Liliput HO-scale model of Zillertalbahn buffet carriage that runs on HOe track.***

*BOTTOM: **Anyone wishing to learn about Austria's railways can do no better than to join the Austrian Railway Group, which produces comprehensive and useful guides about railway activities of specific areas of the country.***

FOR MORE INFORMATION

The first step to learning more about Austria's railways is to join the Austrian Railway Group (ARG), with its excellent website and active email group. Their quarterly magazines contain information about prototype and modelling developments and they produce a very useful series of booklets about rail centres in the country. These items are also available to non-members through their sales stand, which visits a number of model railway exhibitions throughout the year (and also by mail order). The ARG publications are in English, which is useful and to see what is available go to www.austrianrailwaygroup.co.uk. The Austrian National Tourist Office can supply information, maps and brochures about Austria via its comprehensive website at www.austria.info.

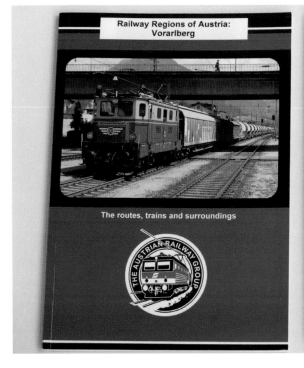

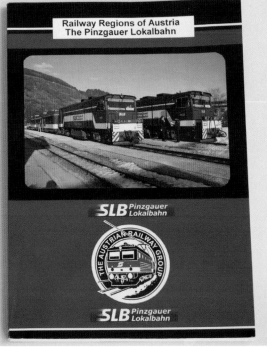

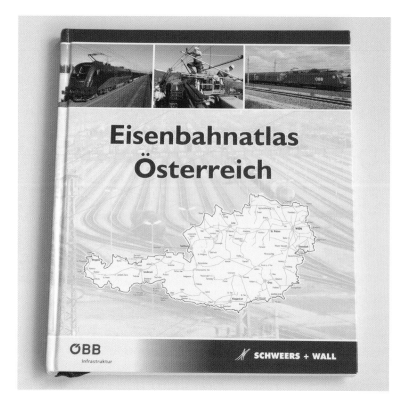

The Schweers + Wall rail atlases are a great way to undertake research about the country. The maps are set out clearly, industrial sidings are shown and if you do not mind carrying them when you go on trains in Europe, they are a great accompaniment to any rail journey.

From the UK, in addition to Austrian Airlines and British Airways, there are budget airlines, including Easyjet and Ryanair, that offer good-value direct flights to Innsbruck, Salzburg, Vienna and some Austrian regional destinations including Linz. Getting to Austria by rail is possible using Eurostar to Brussels or Paris via London St Pancras International station. For an excellent explanation on how to do this go to www.seat61.com/Austria.

DVDS

Austrian Railway Group member Norman Lamb produces a DVD series called *Austrian Railway Memories* that features classic steam excursions, diesel and electric traction on standard- and narrow-gauge lines in Austria taken between 1989 and 1994. These good value-for-money productions are brimming with nostalgia and for more information about the DVDs go to www.austrianrailwaygroup.co.uk, where they can be purchased.

Lineside Video Productions (www.linesidevideos. co.uk) has dedicated productions about Austrian railways in addition to bimonthly DVDs about various European countries. Another good source of DVDs is Ticket to Ride (www.tickettoride.co.uk), which has over twenty-five of its own productions about Austrian railways.

BOOKS AND MAGAZINES

Today's Railways Europe monthly magazine contains regular updates on Austrian railway activities. This magazine is available from many newsagents in the UK and is in the English language.

A superb railway atlas of the country is published by Schweers + Wall (www.railatlas.eu) with 144 pages. The maps are in colour at scale 1:150,000 with various enlargements and there is a station index and an index of railway companies.

An *Austrian Railways* motive power handbook, with full English text, a railway map and colour photographs, is produced by Platform 5 Publishing Ltd. Books on Austrian railways can be obtained from specialized book suppliers such as Platform 5 Publishing (www.platform5.com). Middleton Press produces a hardback book entitled *Austrian Narrow Gauge featuring Steam in the Alps* (www.middletonpress. co.uk).

There are numerous European guidebooks. Some are better than others for rail-oriented travellers. I have found the *Lonely Planet Austria* guide is useful with its accommodation, historical and scenic rail journey information.

Eisenbahn Journal's 'Abenteuer Alpenbahn' layout planning and building magazine special covers the building of layouts and dioramas based on the Austrian Arlberg, the Brenner and the Tauern Alpine passes in HO scale. It is an inspirational publication with its superb photography and layouts depicted. Over the years, *Eisenbahn Journal* and other publications have published superbly illustrated accounts of various Austrian railway highlights such as 'The Arlbergbahn'. These can be viewed at www. vgbahn.info.

A magazine in the German language dedicated to model and prototype Austrian railways is *Modellbahnwelt* (www.modellbahnwelt.at).

WEBSITES

There are a huge number of really useful links on the Austrian Railway Group website. These include model shops in Austria, private railway companies in Austria, model manufacturers, online photo websites and prototype historical information (www. austrianrailwaygroup.co.uk).

Other websites of interest include:

- http://bahnbilder.warumdenn.net/index.php, a superb website that covers all current Austrian locomotive classes
- www.bahn-austria.at, which looks at the large number of models produced for the Austrian market
- www.oebb.at, which contains ÖBB timetables and ticket information; the information is also available in English
- www.alpenbahnen.net, which contains a huge amount of information in words, diagrams and pictures about most Alpine railways
- www.railfaneurope.net/list/austria.html, the Austrian section of the Railfaneurope website,

Those wishing to follow Austrian railways are fortunate in having the Austrian Railway Group as a progressive society in the UK, plus Platform 5 Publishing has Austria as one of its European Motive Power handbooks.

A backpacker looks on enviously as he sees an Austrian Inter-City service that he cannot board because his train pass is limited to local train services only. The HO-scale figures are by Preiser.

which has a wealth of information about Austria's railways; the site also contains an overview of the lines, plus a large number of links to other websites.

EURO-MODELLING INTERLUDE – ST BLASIEN Hʙғ

A multilevel HO-scale layout by Ben Jones.

This new European HO-scale layout under construction by Ben Jones measures 2.7 × 2.2m, with the operator working from the centre of the layout. St Blasien Hbf will be a multilevel continuous layout, with two main decks and connecting inclines using Code 75 Peco track and hidden storage lines. These pictures were taken only days after the baseboards were delivered by White Rose Modelworks. The layout's name is taken from a town in the Black Forest, close to the Swiss border, and reflects Ben's interest in the railways around Basel, which he has been visiting since the late 1990s.

ST BLASIEN Hʙғ LAYOUT PROFILE

Name:	St Blasien Hbf
Type of layout:	multilevel continuous layout with two main decks and connecting inclines
Era:	Epoch V
Location:	southern Black Forest
Scale:	HO
Dimensions:	overall dimensions are 2.7 × 2.2m, with the operator in the centre of the layout
Track:	Peco Code 75
Ballast:	a wide variety of suppliers and colours
Control:	DCC (system TBC)
Locomotives:	Fleischmann, Heljan, Jouef, Liliput, LS Models and Roco
Freight wagons:	Brawa, Fleischmann, Liliput and Roco
Coaching stock:	ACME, Brawa, Liliput, LS Models, Railtop and Roco
Landscaping:	Woodland Scenics, Noch, Busch
Bridges:	Hack-Brücken, Noch
Buildings:	scratch-built, Faller, Noch, Busch
Trees:	Noch, Heki, Woodland Scenics
Figures:	Noch and Preiser
Scenic materials:	Noch, Heki, Woodland Scenics
Building time:	the project commenced in June 2014 and is ongoing.

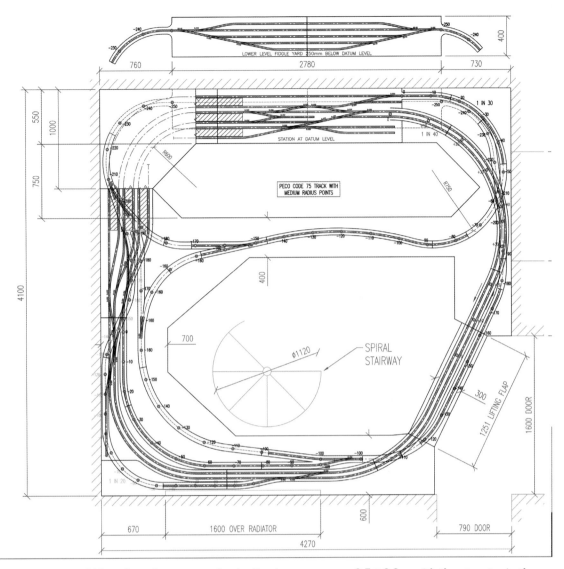

This new European HO scale under construction by Ben Jones measures 2.7 × 2.2m, with the operator in the centre of the layout. BEN JONES/THE GOODS YARD

The St Blasien Hbf HO-scale layout will be a multilevel continuous layout with two main decks and connecting inclines. BEN JONES/ THE GOODS YARD

APPENDICES

APPENDIX I   FIFTEEN WAYS TO LEARN MORE ABOUT YOUR CHOSEN PROTOTYPE

- First, the most valuable way to learn is to visit the area that you have chosen to model if at all possible. This is useful even if the specific railway company you wish to model no longer operates, or if you are modelling an historic period. It is important to gain 'a feel' for the place. What is the landscape like? What vegetation is common in the area? What are the towns and villages like?
- Find out if your chosen country has an enthusiast society in the UK or in Europe. I thoroughly recommend joining that society and ascertaining what publications they have to provide you with good background information about your chosen line or locality.
- Buy at least one issue of a railway modelling magazine of the country that you intend to model. Do this despite any lack of understanding of the language, because the advertisements will prove to be very useful as you learn what products are available for your chosen scale and locality.
- If you do get the opportunity, visit a large model railway show in your country of choice, because there will be a lot of traders there offering an array of products that you may not learn about in any other way. You will also be able to look at layouts of the country that you wish to model.
- Find out what Internet forum groups are available for your chosen country. These are usually free to enroll in and you will soon be making your own posts on the forum even if it is only to ask questions, because in my experience established modellers are very keen to assist beginners. Such forums do not have to be limited to those based in the UK, because there are several European forums that keep me up to date with railway events of my chosen countries.
- Find an Internet translator programme that you like working with and save this as a favourite on

A modern German station in HO scale with a Piko DB Class 642 Desiro. City walls are a common sight in many European towns.

your tablet or PC. While the English translation will not be perfect – partly because there will be a lot of designated railway terms – it will prove to be a lot better than nothing.

- Look out for the media pages on Internet websites of your chosen railway company, because most usually contain press releases in English and though they might relate to current events they are a good way of building up your fund of knowledge.

- Find out what books are available about your chosen subject. Societies sometimes have a lending library of books about their particular country, which can be useful.

- Consider subscribing to UK-based magazines that cover European themes. These include *Continental Modeller* and *Today's Railways Europe*. The former is available as an online purchase either for specific issues or as a regular subscription.

- Look on the Internet or ask the society of your choice if they have a dictionary of railway terms. This will be really helpful as you find your way around the new topic.

- Keep an eye open for model railway layouts of the country you are modelling and endeavour to see these at shows in the UK and chat to the operators. You will soon find that you have much in common with others who have a similar enthusiasm to yours.

- Write to the railway company whose line you are modelling if you have specific enquiries. I have found this to be most productive, because employees of railway companies are often pleased that someone from another country is interested in their employer's history.

- You may be fortunate in establishing friendships with like-minded enthusiasts who will be able to pass on their years of experience in the hobby.

- Tourist offices of countries usually have some information about railway operations on their websites and in their brochures. In addition, information will be available about travel passes for their country. Incidentally, there is an increasing number of holiday regions (in Germany and Switzerland, for example) that provide free local public transport passes for the period of a stay in hotels and apartments that take part in the scheme.

- Each year, there are more and more 'driver's eye-view' DVDs produced to supplement the common 'from the lineside' video productions. These are a good way to learn more about the route that you are modelling.

This Roco model of SBB Cargo Class 203 locomotive has been weathered using weathering dyes. The platform lights are by Beli Beco, the figures by Preiser and platform seats by Kibri. The platform was made from 2mm mounting cardboard.

APPENDIX 2   USEFUL WEBSITES

EUROPEAN RAILWAY OPERATORS

Alpine railways	www.alpenbahnen.net
Austrian narrow gauge	www.noevog.at
Austrian railways	www.oebb.at
Belgian railways	www.belgianrail.be
BLS	www.bls.ch
Czech railways	www.cd.cz
Danish railways	www.dsb.dk
Dutch railways	www.ns.nl
Eurostar	www.eurostar.com
Eurotunnel	www.eurotunnel.com
Finnish railways	www.vr.fi
French railways	www.sncf.com
German railways	www.bahn.de
Greece	www.ose.gr
Hungarian railways	www.mav.hu
Italian railways	www.trenitalia.com
Luxembourg railways	www.cfl.lu
Norwegian railways	www.nsb.no
Polish railways	www.pkp.pl
Portuguese railways	www.cp.pt
Rhätische Bahn	www.rhb.ch
Slovakian railways	www.zsr.sk
Spanish railways	www.renfe.com
Steepest rack railway in the world	www.pilatus.com
Swedish railways	www.sj.se
Swiss railways	www.sbb.ch
Thalys rail services	www.thalys.com

MODEL ROLLING STOCK (MANUFACTURERS AND SEVERAL RETAILERS)

Arnold/Lima/Jouef/ Rivarossi	www.hornbyinternational.com
Austrian narrow gauge	www.ferro-train.com
Bahnhof Europa (retailer)	www.gaugemaster.com
Bemo	www.bemo-modellbahn.de
Brawa	www.brawa.de
Contikits (secondhand specialist)	www.contikits.com
Golden Valley Hobbies (retailer)	www.goldenvalleyhobbies.co.uk
Hag	www.hag.ch
Fleischmann	www.fleischmann.de
Heljan	www.heljan.dk

Jägerndorfer	www.jaegerndorfer.at
Lenz DCC	www.lenz.com
LGB	www.lgb.de
Liliput	www.liliput.de
Märklin (and Z gauge)	www.maerklin.com
Mehano	www.mehano.si
Piko	www.piko.de
Roco	www.roco.cc
Tillig	www.tillig.com
Trix (and Minitrix)	www.trix.de
Winco (European specialist retailer)	www.winco.uk.com

SCENICS

4D Model Shop	www.modelshop.co.uk
Anita Décor	www.anitadecor.nl
Auhagen	www.auhagen.de
Busch	www.busch-model.com
Double O Scenics	www.doubleoscenics.weebly.com
Faller/Pola	www.faller.de
Hedgerow Scenics	www.hedgerowscenics.co.uk
Heki	www.heki-kittler.de
International Models	www.internationalmodels.net
Langmesser Modellwelt	www.langmesser-modellwelt.de
miniNatur	www.mininatur.de
Model Scene	www.model-scene.com
Model Tree Shop	www.themodeltreeshop.co.uk
Noch	www.noch.com
Sommerfeldt catenary	www.sommerfeldt.de
Train Terrain	www.trainterrainmodels.co.uk
Treemendus	www.treemendus-scenics.co.uk
Viessmann and Kibri	www.viessmann-modell.com
WW Scenics	www.wwscenics.co.uk

INSPIRING PERMANENT EXHIBITIONS

Bergun exhibition and museum	www.bahnmuseum-albula.ch
Black Forest line	www.schwarzwald-modell-bahn.de
Hamburg exhibition (world's biggest)	www.miniatur-wunderland.de
French attraction in Lyon	www.miniworld-lyon.com
Rotterdam	www.miniworldrotterdam.com
Swiss exhibition in Fribourg	www.kaeserberg.ch

TRAVEL, RESEARCH

European Railway Server	www.railfaneurope.net
European Train Enthusiasts (USA)	www.ete.org

This HO-scale video cameraman is still busy getting footage of an ÖBB Class 5022 two-car DMU by Piko that is just about to leave the station. The fern to the right is a laser-cut card plant by Langmesser Modellwelt.

Miniature Wunderland in Hamburg is the world's largest permanent model railway attraction. It is popular with visitors of all ages. Here is just one corner of their Alpine display.

Maps and guidebooks	www.stanfords.co.uk
Rail tickets for Europe	www.voyages-sncf.com
Rail travel guides	www.bradt-travelguides.com
The Man in Seat Sixty-One (a wealth of information)	www.seat61.com

SOCIETIES

Austrian Railway Group	www.austrianrailwaygroup.co.uk
Benelux Railways Society	www.beneluxrailways.co.uk
European Railways Association	www.eurorail.org.uk
German Railway Society	www.grs-uk.org
Historical German Railway Group	www.azg.org.uk
Iberian Railways Society	www.iberianrailwayssociety.org
Italian Railway Society	www.italianrailways.co.uk

N Gauge Society (World Wide Group)	www.ngaugesociety.com
Scandinavian Railways Society	www.scanrailsoc.org.uk
SNCF Society	www.sncfsociety.org.uk
A Swiss enthusiast group in the Netherlands	www.spoorgroepzwitserland.nl
Swiss Railways Society	www.swissrailsoc.org.uk

*These lists are the main sources known to the author and are not claimed to be complete.

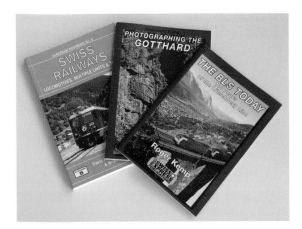 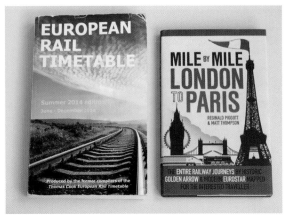

ABOVE LEFT: *Some countries are easier to research than others. One of the greatest hurdles to finding out more about your chosen country is simply knowing who publishes what about the country. The Platform 5 Motive Power handbooks are published for Austria, Benelux, France, Ireland, Italy, Germany and Switzerland. The two books to the right are publications of the Swiss Railways Society.*

ABOVE RIGHT: *Travel books and railway timetables are a great way to spend a winter's evening in the armchair, or better still to be in your rucksack as you travel on Europe's railways.*

ABOVE LEFT: *There are a number of good-quality railway modelling magazines published in France including,* **Loco-Revue** *and* **RMF**.

ABOVE RIGHT: *It's an O-scale cheerio from the world of modelling European railways. This picture was taken at Bauma 2014 Kleinseries model railway exhibition in Switzerland.*

INDEX